Sustainable Living

For Home, Neighborhood and Community

Save Energy • Save Resources
Save Money • Live Better

Mick Winter

Westsong Publishing
Napa, California

Writing noted
on page 37
12-2011

Printed in the United States of America.

First Edition

Library of Congress Control Number: 2006940827

ISBN-13: 978-0-9659000-5-8

Westsong Publishing
PO Box 2254
Napa CA 94558
www.westsongpublishing.com

Cover illustration by Helle Bro Clemmensen

To Sophia, who craftily conceals her wisdom,

to Minka, A-Choo, Puss (I & II) and Boots—it all looked sustainable to them,

and to Sally and Narc, who probably didn't give it much thought.

About this book

Sustainable Living: For Home, Neighborhood and Community was written to provide sustainable living information based on the assumption that our society, its resources and institutions will continue on more or less as things are going now.

If you believe that our society might be subject to some rather disruptive influences, you might consider buying *Peak Oil Prep: Three Things You Can Do to Prepare for Peak Oil, Climate Change and Economic Collapse,* an expanded version of this book by the same author. It is available at: **www.PeakOilPrep.com**.

All links in this book to websites, books, DVDs, products and other information are available at:

www.sustainablelivingbook.com

These online links are checked and updated regularly to ensure their accuracy and functionality

You can also buy additional copies of this book at the above website.

"I am at two with nature."

Woody Allen

Table of Contents

Introduction

What is Sustainable Living?

...and why would you want to do it?

Webster's *New Millennium Dictionary* defines *sustainable living* as

**"any lifestyle based on energy-saving
and environmental responsibility"**

Wikipedia.org defines it as "a lifestyle that could, hypothetically, be sustained unmodified for many generations without exhausting any natural resources." It further says "The term can be applied to individuals or societies. Its adherents most often hold true sustainability as a goal or guide, and make lifestyle tradeoffs favoring sustainability where practical."

Wikipedia says that these tradeoffs "involve transport, housing, energy, and diet" and states that Lester R. Brown, founder of the Earth Policy Institute, concisely summarizes the situation as "sustaining progress depends on shifting from a fossil fuel-based, automobile-centered, throwaway economy to a renewable energy-based, diversified transport, reuse/recycle economy."

What do these definitions come down to? Sustainable living is a goal, one that can never be totally realized in an industrialized, developed society, but one that can certainly be attempted. And the more we strive toward that goal, the better off we, our society and our planet are.

In fact, some say that sustainability is not enough. That what we need to do is go *beyond* sustainability, to begin restoring the planet. This is presumably impossible to do with such resources as fossil fuels, but we can begin to restore our air, our water and our soil.

North Americans, and to a lesser extent most members of other developed countries, have an advantage in trying to live more sustainable lives. The reason? There is already a huge amount of excess in our lives. Excess energy use, excess water use, excess food use, excess *stuff*.

Ecological footprint

The "ecological footprint" of a human on the earth is measured by the amount of biologically productive area (land and sea) needed to support the person. The unit is called a "global hectare" (or "global acre") and it represents an average of all productive area on Planet Earth. In industrial countries, that footprint (number of global hectares needed to support a person) is high; in many "undeveloped" countries that footprint is far smaller.

For example, the ecological footprint of someone in the United States, on the average, is about 24. (Only the United Arab Emirates is higher, with a footprint of 25.9) That means that 24 biologically productive acres around the world are necessary to support that one person with their food, transportation, shelter, goods and services.

In Afghanistan, however, the ecological footprint is 0.2, which means that the average person needs—at their current level—to be supported by only 0.2 global hectares over the course of a year.

Worldwide, based on the current population of the planet, there exist only 4.5 biologically productive acres per person. That means that for everyone on the planet to live at the current level of the average American, we would need 5.5 planets.

Here's a list of selected national footprints:

Country	Ecological Footprint
United Arab Emirates	25.9
United States	24.0
Canada	18.5
Kuwait	18.0
Australia	17.3
Finland	16.8
New Zealand	14.8
United Kingdom	13.8
Sweden	13.6
Japan	10.6
Mexico	5.9
Bolivia	4.9
Cuba	4.2
Vietnam	2.0
Afghanistan	0.2

Global Footprint Network
www.footprintnetwork.org

For more information on world and national ecological footprints.

Ecological Footprint Quiz
www.myfootprint.org
Calculate your own footprint.

The high "footprint" in highly-developed (perhaps even *over-developed?*) countries gives us a lot of slack, and room to cut back on our use of energy and natural resources. But why would we want to do that?

Many environmentalists feel that those individuals who are the most committed to the health of the planet and the lives of future generations are already living their lives as sustainably as possible. Unfortunately, it's a very small minority. It's the rest of us who need to make changes in order to improve the state of the planet. Those of us who may care, but who just haven't seen how we can afford to be "sustainable".

But why should we even want to live sustainably? Why should we do without the things and lifestyle we're used to into order to supposedly benefit some abstract future? After all, U.S. Vice-President Dick Cheney said that "the American way of life is non-negotiable". Wasn't he speaking for most of us when he said that? Why should we give up anything?

Save money, help the planet

Well, the pleasant surprise for many of us is that because of the excess and slack built into our system, we really don't have to give up much, if anything, in order to live sustainably. In fact, by living a more sustainable lifestyle, we can *gain* a lot.

You don't have to live more sustainably for the sake of the planet; just do it for yourself.

- Use less energy and you **save money** on your utility bills. It's a bonus that using less energy helps society and the planet.
- Use less gasoline and you **save money** by going to the gas station less frequently. It's a bonus that you slow down depletion of fossil fuels and help in a small way to lessen air pollution.

- Grow some of your own food and you **save money**, get a little exercise, and are able to eat healthier food. It's a bonus that the use of petroleum-based pesticides and natural gas-based fertilizers is lessened, that less food has to be transported long distances by polluting, highway-clogging trucks, and that less packaging is needed for the food you eat.

- Walk or ride a bicycle more, and drive less, and you **save money** on gasoline, wear-and-tear on your car (that means fewer costly repairs and you extend the life of your car), and get healthier. It's a bonus that you help reduce air pollution, and slow down fossil fuel depletion.

- Use less water in your home—in the kitchen, the bathroom, and your yard—and you **save money** on your water bill. It's a bonus that the water you don't use helps keep aquifers at a higher level, can be used for growing food, and helps contribute to healthy rivers.

- Use less gas, oil or electricity for heating your home or the hot water you use, and you **save money** on your utility bills. It's a bonus that you use fewer fossil fuel resources and lessen the need for new power plants.

- Use less electricity for lighting your home, and you **save money** on light bulbs and electricity bills. It's a bonus that you again lessen the need for new, probably polluting, power plants.

- Share tools with your neighbors and you all **save money** by not needing your own separate set of tools and not having to hire someone to do repairs or maintenance on your home. It's a bonus that the fewer tools you buy, the less resources that are used by society to produce and transport those tools.

- Share errands needing a car with neighbors and you **save money** on gasoline. It's a bonus that the result is less air pollution, and decreased use of fossil fuel.

Starting to see a pattern here? You don't need to do these things for the planet or the environment. Do them for *yourself* —and your family. The environmental benefits just naturally and automatically follow. Your motivation doesn't even matter.

By using less fossil fuel energy and fewer resources, you'll save money. Potentially lots of money. You'll probably eat healthier and get healthier. You'll have more contact with your family and your neighbors. And, yes, you can likely even enjoy life more. All this and, as a bonus and without any sacrifice, you'll be helping the planet and the environment as well.

Not a bad deal, eh?

Can you buy yourself green?

There are many websites, magazines and newspaper articles telling you how you can live "greener" by buying things. Buy this refrigerator or this article of clothing or this car or this new home or this amazing new gadget and you'll be a greener or more sustainable person.

That isn't what this book is about. Yes, there are "things" that are more sustainable than "other things". But most of us don't need *more* things, we need *fewer* things. So we'll try to minimize the number of things we mention in the book that you can buy for sustainability reasons.

This also isn't a book about buying or building a new "green" home. We assume that you, like most others, are staying where you are, or someplace similar, and that you just want to know how you can save money and energy in your present, standard designed and built, home. We assume that you don't want to spend *more* money; you want to spend *less* money.

We think this book will help.

Top Three

With three simple actions, you can make a major change in your energy use, personal health, and well-being. If millions of us did these actions, it would make a major change not only in our own but in our country's well-being. All three actions require little, if any, cost and will produce results very quickly.

Replace light bulbs

The most important and effective energy-saving and money-saving thing you can do in your home or office is to replace incandescent light bulbs with compact fluorescent light bulbs.

Incandescent bulbs are basically little heaters that also produce light. They make light by passing electricity through a small wire (*filament*). The wire heats up and glows, producing light. Unfortunately only 10% of the energy they use produces light; the other 90% produces heat. This is a very serious waste of energy.

Compact fluorescent (CF) bulbs pass electricity through a gas-charged tube. The chemical reaction produces the light. The bulb remains cooler and produces more light (measured in *lumens*) than incandescent bulbs, with less power. The average CF bulb uses 66-75% less electricity to produce the same amount of light as an incandescent bulb.

When you use less energy for your lighting, you save money. You save money because you use less electricity. Using less electricity means you're ultimately using fewer fossil fuels, such as the oil, gas or coal used in power plants. You're helping conserve those fossil fuels, and you're helping to prevent the air pollution they produce when burned.

It has been estimated that if every U.S. household replaced just one 60-watt incandescent light bulb with a CF bulb, the pollution reduction would be equivalent to removing one million cars from the road. Think how it would be if we all replaced *all* of our bulbs.

Coming Up: Keep your eyes out for LED (Light-Emitting Diode) light bulbs. They're not yet at the low-cost stage of CF bulbs, but they will be. And they offer far greater energy efficiency and longevity.

Advantages of CF bulbs

Long Lasting - While CF bulbs cost more than incandescent, they can last anywhere from 8,000 to 15,000 hours, compared to the typical 1,000 for an incandescent bulb.

Money Saving - If you replace a 100-watt incandescent bulb with a 32-watt CF bulb (which provides the same amount of light), you can save at least $32 over the life of the bulb. Replace 10 bulbs in your home, and that's a savings of more than $300. A bulb can pay for itself with normal use in just five months.

Cool - CF bulbs are also cool to the touch, with a temperature of less than 100° F.

Rebates - Many utility companies offer rebates or even free bulbs to homeowners. Check to see if your local company has these offers.

Selection of shades – CF bulbs are available in several shades of light, ranging from bluish to golden or bright sunlight. Pick the ones best suited for your purposes.

For inside and outside -- CF bulbs are designed for either indoor and outdoor use. Check the package to make sure you get the kind you need.

> **Hint**
>
> Remember "Watt Four" — CF bulbs use about ¼ of the wattage as incandescent bulbs to produce the same amount of light (lumens). So as a rule of thumb, replace an old incandescent bulb with a CF bulb of about ¼ the wattage, i.e. replace a 60-watt with a 15-watt.

Walk—or ride a bike

- Helps with air pollution
- Saves fossil fuels
- Saves you money
- Improves your health

There are so many benefits to walking or bike riding that this book has room to list only a few. The physical exercise from moving your body will increase your blood flow, strengthen all the muscles in your body, loosen your joints, improve your breathing, help you lose weight over time, and increase your appetite yet help you be satisfied with lower food intake.

Your mental outlook will improve and emotionally you'll feel more positive. You'll also be able to get outdoors, see your neighbors and the neighborhood, enjoy nature, reduce auto pollution, save money on gas, and feel the pleasure of being outside in the air. And it's all free.

Note: If you absolutely can't get along without driving, at least drive *less*. Here are some tips on how to do this:

- Combine trips. Wait to combine a number of errands into one trip
- Telecommute at least once a week
- Carpool or use public transit whenever possible
- Share errands with neighbors

Walkable Communities

It's much easier, safer, and more enjoyable to walk in a town when it's a walkable community. "Walkable" simply means that it's designed for the enjoyment—and safety—of people, not only for the unobstructed movement of cars.

> **How Can I Find and Help Build a Walkable Community?**
> www.walkable.org/article1.htm
>
> **Article by walkable community advocate Dan Burden.**

Is your community walkable? Here are Dan Burden's 10 keys to walkable, living communities.   How well does your community rate in each category?

1. Compact, lively town center.
2. Many linkages to neighborhoods (including walkways, trails and roadways).
3. Low speed streets (in downtown and neighborhoods, 20-25 mph common).
4. Neighborhood schools and parks.
5. Public places packed with children, teenagers, older adults, and people with disabilities.
6. Convenient, safe, and easy street crossings.
7. Inspiring and well-maintained public streets.
8. Land use and transportation mutually beneficial.
9. Celebrated public space and public life.
10. Many people walking.

> **10 Keys to Walkable/Living Communities**
> www.lgc.org/freepub/land_use/articles/ten_keys/page01.html
>
> **Full article on the 10 keys above.**

> **Walkable Communities, Inc.**
> www.walkable.org
> Dan Burden's website dedicated to helping communities become more walkable and pedestrian friendly.
>
> **Center for Livable Communities**
> www.lgc.org/center
> California's Local Government Commission.

Ride a bike

Bicycles are one of the great inventions of the world. As John Ryan's book *Seven Wonders: Everyday Things for a Healthier Planet* says:

"The Bicycle: The most energy efficient form of travel ever invented and the world's most popular transport vehicle".

Pound for pound, a person on a bicycle expends less energy than any creature or machine covering the same distance. A bike is always handy for the one out of four car trips in the United States that are less than a mile. As with walking, you'll:

- Help with air pollution
- Save fossil fuels
- Save money
- Improve your health

> **Bicycle**
> http://en.wikipedia.org/wiki/Bicycle
> From Wikipedia.
>
> **Bikeability Checklist**
> www.bicyclinginfo.org/cps/checklist.htm
> How bikeable is your community?

Zap
www.zapworld.com

Zap sells electric bikes and kits for converting your standard bike into an electrified power assist bike.

Bike Web Site
www.bikewebsite.com

Bicycle tune-up and repair for all types of bikes, with lots of illustrations.

Jim Langley
www.jimlangley.net

Wonderful site on everything about bicycles, including buying one, using it and repairing it. From the former technical editor of Bicycling magazine.

Park Tool
www.parktool.com/repair

Detailed instructions on bicycle repair and maintenance, with illustrations.

Plant a garden

Plant a garden in your yard (page 74) or start a community garden (page 85). Either way, you'll have a source of free, healthy vegetables and herbs, and you'll get exercise outside in the fresh air.

Home

HOUSEHOLD

After the mortgage or rent, gas and electricity are likely the biggest expenses in your home. Do the following three things and you'll have taken the biggest and easiest cost-cutting measures that you can take in your home.

Replace incandescent light bulbs with compact fluorescent bulbs

(See page 17.)

Disconnect all electrical items when not in use

Few people realize just how much electricity many appliances can consume when they're not actually being used but are still plugged in. Such appliances are called "energy vampires" or "phantom appliances". These include radios and television sets, VCRs, home entertainment systems, battery chargers (for cell phones, cameras, music players), computers, printers, photocopiers, and even kitchen appliances.

The U.S. Department of Energy estimates that 75% of the electricity used to power home electronics is consumed *while the products are turned off*. This can be avoided by unplugging the appliance, or by using a power strip so that when you turn the power strip off you cut all power to the appliance.

Obviously you'll want to keep some appliances plugged in if, for example, they're dependent on maintaining an accurate clock to carry out their function and they don't have an internal battery to do that. But others can be unplugged between use.

To find out how much electricity each of your appliances consumes, even when it's not actively being used, we suggest that you buy a *Kill-a-Meter*, an electricity usage monitor.

Turn down thermostats and water heater temperature

Thermostat

Reducing temperatures saves electricity and/or gas and the fossil fuels required to produce them. It also saves you money. On the average, every 2° F. lower on your thermostat will save 2% on your heating bill. Conserve further by turning down the heat at night and while you are away from your home—or by installing a programmable thermostat.

Water Heater

The water heater uses more energy than any other device in the home. Most water heaters are kept at the factory-set temperature of 140°-145°. The expense of maintaining a tankful of water at this temperature, 24 hours a day, is very high. The high temperature also a safety hazard if you have small children in the home.

Turn the temperature down to 120°, your water will still be hot enough for showers, dish washing (most new automatic dishwashers raise the temperature themselves, if necessary), and clothes washing. The lower temperature will use a lot less gas or electricity, and save you a lot of money. If, for some reason, you find that 120° is too low for your purposes, you can always set it a little higher.

Note: An even better solution, but one that requires an expense, is converting your always-on water heater to a tankless device that heats water on-demand. These have been standard in Europe and other parts of the world for decades, and are slowly becoming common in the United States.

More

- In the winter, change or clean your furnace air filters once a month - The heater has to use more energy when the filter is full of dust.
- Insulate your home against heat loss and periodically check the insulation
- Weather-strip and caulk to minimize air leaks
- Turn your computer off when you're not using it - It will reduce wear on the computer, and save energy and money. If you have to leave the computer on, at least turn the monitor off. CRT monitors use more than half of the system's energy (LCD monitors are much better).
- A laptop computer uses up to 90% less energy than a desktop computer.

> **Home Energy Saver**
>
> http://hes.lbl.gov/
> Do-it-yourself energy audit tool from Lawrence Berkeley National Laboratory.

KITCHEN

Conserving in the kitchen means using electricity and gas less, and hands and muscles more. Modern kitchens are filled with "labor saving" devices. But they're not money and energy saving.

Unplug appliances not being used

(See page 23.)

Switch to hand-operated appliances and tools

Get rid of the electric juicer, can opener, and whatever else you have that does what could be done almost as easily by hand.

Use solar cooking whenever possible

(See page 101.)

More

- Don't preheat your oven. That's necessary only for baking breads and pastries.
- Turn off the stove burners 2-3 minutes (and the oven 10 minutes) before the end of cooking time. The food will continue to cook and you'll save money.
- Electric kettles use much less energy than a stove burner when heating water. Clean the kettle regularly with boiling water and vinegar and you'll remove the mineral deposits inside, improving the taste of the water and making the kettle more energy efficient.
- Use small appliances such as toaster ovens or microwaves to cook or re-heat small amounts of food. They'll use up to 50% less energy than your oven.

- Skip the pre-rinse for your dishwasher and you'll save up to 20 gallons of water per load.
- Scrape off dishes instead of rinsing them. Most new dishwashers can handle this. Run the dishwasher only when it's full.
- Your refrigerator uses more energy than any other home appliance. Keep your refrigerator coils clean (at least every year and preferably every six months), don't keep the refrigerator jam packed with food (although this helps the freezer), and keep the refrigerator set between 37º-42º F. and the freezer between 0º and 5º F.
- Water boils faster if there's a lid on the pan. Once it's boiling, turn it down to a light boil instead of a rolling boil. The temperature will be just as hot.
- Thaw frozen foods before cooking; they'll need less energy to cook.
- Food cooks faster in glass dishes than metal ones.
- Pressure cookers use very little energy and cook very quickly. If you're afraid of them from earlier days, don't worry. The new ones are much easier—and safer —to use.

BATHROOM

The best ways to conserve in the bathroom are by using less water and particularly less hot water (page 24).

Turn the faucet off

When brushing your teeth or washing your face, turn the water off except when you actually need it. You can save several gallons of water each time.

Use a low-flow toilet

If you have a regular toilet, replace it with a low-flow toilet. Many municipalities offer free replacements, including the labor. At the very least, put in water displacement bags to lessen the amount of water the tank actually holds.

Use a low-flow shower head

Replace any normal shower heads with low-flow. They're inexpensive, and some municipalities even give them away for free. You can reduce water usage by almost 50% and save water-heating money as well.

Don't flush

For urine only, it's not necessary to flush each time. Save the water for when it's essential. As they used to say in California during the 1970s drought, "Brown goes down, but yellow is mellow."

Shower together

They liked this one in California.

Switch to composting toilets

With one flush of your toilet you're using more water than a majority of people in the world have access to in an entire day. And in most cases, you're flushing not just water, but *drinking* water.

Composting toilets save huge amounts of water, since they never use *any*. The human manure ends up as compost—in a safe, sanitary and non-smelly method.

Composting Toilet
http://en.wikipedia.org/wiki/Composting_toilet

From Wikipedia.

Composting Toilet World
www.compostingtoilet.org

Extensive information from Envirolet, a manufacturer of composting toilets.

Build Your Own Humanure Toilet
www.jenkinspublishing.com/sawdustoilet.html

Complete instructions for a $25 toilet.

Humanure Handbook
www.weblife.org/humanure

A guide to composting human manure. The entire book online—free! Great book, great deal. Consider, however, buying a copy of the book for convenience and to support the author.

The Toilet Papers

Book on recycling waste and conserving water. A classic that's back in print. It's by Sim van der Ryn, well-known sustainable architect and former official California State Architect.

Use alternatives to toilet paper

The following aren't so much recommendations as they are suggestions in case you have to deal with a *lack* of toilet paper.

Hint: The Romans used a sponge attached to the end of a stick which soaked in a bucket of brine, early Americans used corncobs and, later, newspapers. Caution: Corncobs and newspaper would not be handled well by a flush toilet.

Toilet Paper
http://en.wikipedia.org/wiki/Toilet_paper
An overview of toilet paper, from Wikipedia.

The Hand/Water Method
www.getlostmagazine.com/features/2000/0004hygiene/hygiene.html
The standard method used throughout much of the world.

Investigating TP Alternatives
www.clarkschpiell.com/home/asswipe.shtml
Some imaginative, and even amusing, alternatives.

Where's the Toilet Paper?
http://bosp.kcc.hawaii.edu/DiamondJournals/Diamondspring03/Wheres_TP.html
A commentary.

The Great Toilet Paper Shortage
http://home.nycap.rr.com/useless/toilet_paper/index.html
Interesting historical information.

LAUNDRY ROOM

Doing laundry the modern way requires water and electricity or gas. The way to save money is to use less of all of them.

Set water heater to 120° F

(See page 24.)

Wash laundry with full loads

The optimal and most economical use of water and electricity is to wash only full loads of laundry ("full" as determined by the washer manufacturer; don't cram the laundry in the washer). Smaller loads use just as much electricity, and often more water than necessary, even with water volume set on a partial amount.

Use a clothesline

Use a clothesline rather than an electric or gas dryer. If the weather outside isn't warm enough to dry your clothes, use an indoor clothesline or clothes dryer rack. You'll save money on energy, and your clothes will last longer.

More

- Wash clothes in cold water. You'll save on water heating costs, and studies show clothes get just as clean in most washers.
- If you use a clothes dryer, dry loads of clothing consecutively. This way you take advantage of the heat from the previous load. Be sure to clean the lint trap after each use.

YARD

Your yard can be transformed into a cornucopia of food. It just takes a little work.

Plant a garden

(See page 74.)

Plant trees

Particularly nut and fruit trees (page 117).

Convert your lawns into gardens

The best thing you can do is rip out your lawns—which are heavy users of water—and replace them with gardens. Food is more important than trying to pass off your home as an English manor house.

There are three basic methods for removing a lawn:
- Use a hoe and spade to scrape away the turf, then turn the soil.
- Use a spade and remove the turf in pieces, cutting roots along the way.
- Cover the grass with newspaper, then cover the paper with six inches or so of topsoil. Some months later the grass will have died off and decomposed. (This method is obviously easier, but takes much longer.)

> **Converting Lawns to Gardens**
> www.backyardnature.net/simple/lawn2gar.htm
>
> **Lawns to Gardens**
> www.yougrowgirl.com/lawns_gardens_convert.php

Depave

Rid the world of a small piece (at least) of concrete and let the earth breathe again. If you absolutely think you have to have something besides grass on which to park and drive your car, at least use ecological permeable pavers that still let the earth breathe and rainwater return to the aquifer.

> **Depaving the World**
> www.culturechange.org/issue10/rregister.html
>
> **How to remove asphalt or concrete from your driveway or the strip between sidewalk and curb. Turn the newly-freed space into vegetables or flowers. Then, look around town for bigger spaces.**

Use a hand lawn mower

If you're not converting all your lawns into vegetable gardens, at least switch over to a hand-powered lawn mower. You'll save money, get some exercise, and reduce energy use and air pollution. If you can't use a hand mower, at least switch over to an electric mower. They don't pollute, and are a lot quieter than gas-powered mowers.

Gas-powered lawn mowers are a major source of air pollution. So much so that many municipalities have programs to help you replace your gas mower with an electric one.

SHELTER

Shared housing, in one form or another, offers perhaps the most sensible and easiest way to cut shelter costs.

Greening your home--that is, making it healthier and more sustainable—saves money and energy.

Building homes of natural, sustainable materials, designed and engineered for minimal energy use and maximum comfort, makes both economic and aesthetic sense.

Share housing with others

Shared housing decreases the cost (and use of resources) per person, and increases the opportunities for social interaction and shared work and responsibility.

There are a number of types of "sharing" housing. Even the nuclear family home can be seen as shared housing— although an "extended" nuclear family with as many people as you can handle makes more sense. Boarding houses (also called "rooming houses") are another way people share housing.

Communal living, where a group of perhaps unrelated people live together in one house, or in a cluster of houses, has been popular for a long time.

There are also ecovillages and intentional communities. (You can find more information on them at page 69.)

One of the most interesting forms of shared housing is "cohousing", where people don't share homes but do share common facilities.

Cohousing

Cohousing is collaborative housing that attempts to overcome the alienation of modern subdivisions where people don't know their neighbors, and there is no sense of community.

It's characterized by private dwellings with their own kitchen, living-dining room, etc, but also extensive common facilities. The common building may include a large dining room, kitchen, lounges, meeting rooms, recreation facilities, library, workshops, childcare.

Usually, cohousing communities are designed and managed by the residents, and are intentional *neighborhoods*. The people are consciously committed to living as a community and the physical design itself encourages and facilitates social contact.

The typical cohousing community has 20 to 30 single family homes along a pedestrian street or clustered around one or more courtyards. Residents of cohousing communities often have at least several (optional) group meals in the common building each week.

This type of housing began in Denmark in the late 1960s, and spread to North America in the late 1980s. There are now more than 80 cohousing communities across the continent, with many more in progress.

Cohousing [book]
Author: Kathryn McCamant

A contemporary approach to housing ourselves.

Senior Cohousing [book]
Author: Charles Durrett

Designing cohousing communities for senior living.

Cohousing Association of the United States
www.cohousing.org

Community list, products and services, resources, news.

Cohousing Company
www.cohousingco.com

The people that pioneered cohousing in North America.

Green your home

Sustainable Living is filled with ideas on how to make *living* in your home more sustainable. But there are also many things you can do to make your home *physically* more sustainable. With a number of physical changes, renovations and additions to your home, it can be healthier, more cost-efficient, less demanding of resources, and a more pleasant place to live.

We don't have room to list the many things you can do, but we do have room to highly recommend this book:

> **Natural Remodeling for the Not-So-Green House [book]**
> **Author: Carol Venolia**
>
> **Greening begins at home. How to renovate your home to make it more environmentally-friendly. From simple to large-scale remedies.**

Build green

It's best if we stop *building* homes. Although we need homes, we have enough buildings. We need to *renovate* the buildings we have and turn them into healthy, comfortable, energy-efficient homes.

That said—and even though we said in this book's introduction that we'd avoid sustainable actions that cost much--if you're going to go ahead and build a home, make sure that at least you've done everything you can in its design, siting, and materials to make it as healthy and sustainable as possible. (And if you're a developer putting up a whole bunch of homes, please *don't* do *cul de sacs*, and please *do* include locally-owned stores, restaurants and other services in each neighborhood. If the city won't let you do mixed-use development, don't do the development.)

A Pattern Language: Towns, Buildings, Construction [book]
Author: Christopher Alexander

Architect Christopher Alexander's almost legendary opus on the elements that make a building or an entire town truly human.

Pattern Language
www.patternlanguage.com

We also highly recommend Alexander's website. You'll find lots of information and resources, including his most recent books.

Alternative Construction [book]
Author: Lynne Elizabeth

Contemporary natural building methods.

The House to Ourselves [book]
Author: Todd Lawson

Reinventing home once the kids are grown. Excellent resource for baby boomers and other empty-nesters, including those who want to live with friends in homes especially designed for groups..

Living Homes [book]
Author: Thomas J. Elpel

Sustainable architecture and design.

The New Ecological Home [book]
Author: Dan Chiras
A complete guide to green building options.

The New Natural House Book [book]
Author: David Pearson

Creating a healthy, harmonious and ecologically sound home.

Alternative building materials

Earthship

Tires + dirt = housing. Now doesn't that seem like a good way to recycle the millions of junked tires scattered around the country?

> Earthship
> www.earthship.org
> Recycled automobile tires filled with compacted earth to form a rammed earth brick encased in steel belted rubber.

Rammed Earth

They're just dirt houses. How can they hold up? Actually, homes made of rammed earth hold up fine, and have for centuries. New techniques of construction make them even more solid and easier to work with, and they provide year-round insulation, quiet and comfort. Plus, they just *feel* good.

> Rammed Earth Works
> www.rammedearthworks.com
> Pioneering California company that also invented the PISÉ (Pneumatically Impacted Stabilized Earth) process.
>
> The Rammed Earth House [book]
> Author: David Easton
> Excellent book by rammed earth pioneer.

Straw bale

"But can't wolves blow down houses made of straw? I seem to remember a story about that." Not these. They're solid. And easy to shape into the type of structure you want. A great way to recycle straw.

The New Straw Bale Home [book]
Author: Catherine Wanek

Good coffee table book that will leave you wanting to build your own.

Serious Straw Bale [book]
Author: Paul Lacinski

A Home Construction guide for all climates.

Strawbale Central
www.strawbalecentral.com

Information on many different natural building techniques.

Strawbale.com
www.strawbale.com

Good information and resources including DVDs.

Family

TOGETHERNESS

Families today spend little time together these days. It's a shame, because they miss out on a lot.

Eat together

One of the saddest things about current American life is that less than half of families have—or take—the time to eat together. Whether because of work, sports, friends, entertainment, shopping or second jobs, many people eat on the run, often alone or elsewhere, such as at fast-food restaurants.

Eating together as a family, usually at dinner, is not just some nice old-fashioned idea that might have worked fifty years ago but is no longer appropriate for today. The family—and by this we mean those living together in a home, whether blood-related or not—is a core unit of society. The more stable the family is, the more stable society is. It's clear that both are pretty shaky these days.

Cook together, eat together, talk together, listen to one another, support one another. It will make a difference. And help make your home a special place for all of you.

Entertain together

In the 1930s in the United States, families would gather around the *one* radio in the home and listen to comedy, news and drama programs. Today you may have a TV in every room, but that doesn't mean there isn't value in coming together and doing something together at least once a week.

We don't suggest that the family comes together by *edict*, but rather by *attraction*. Find things that family members actually enjoy and want to do. We'll leave the possibilities up to you, but they might include such things as playing cards and games, listening to—or making—music, reading books aloud, making crafts, hiking, pursuing hobbies, or discussing current events. You can probably come up with more creative ideas based on the interests of your own family.

Does this sound corny to us jaded 21st century people? Maybe. Is it still a good idea? You bet.

Hold weekly meetings

We're not talking about a meeting where Mom and Dad gather everyone together, pretend to take input from the kids, assign jobs, and then dismiss everyone after having a cup of hot cocoa. (Actually, the cocoa's not a bad idea.)

The reality is that a huge number of homes don't have both Mom and Dad, and many others don't have either. But it's still important that everyone that *does* live in the household gathers together weekly to discuss how the household is going, to clear the air of any gripes and misunderstandings, and to set goals that will benefit everyone. Let family members take turns running the meetings to lessen the possibility of any one person always controlling them, and to ensure that there is a variety of opinions and creative ideas. It will also give the kids good experience in running meetings.

PETS

Pets can live sustainably, too—although your cat may grumble.

Grow your own catnip

Fluffy needs a little stress relief and entertainment, too. You can grow all she needs.

> Grow Your Own Catnip
> http://home.ivillage.com/pets/cats/0,,hkp2,00.html

Make your own pet food

Save money and give them healthier food. For example, here's a recipe for cat treats.

- 1 1/2 cups rolled oats
- 1/4 cup vegetable oil
- 1/2 cup flour
- 1/2 cup tuna oil, chicken broth or beef bouillon

Preheat oven to 350° F. Mix all ingredients into a dough. Dust hands with flour and form small, 1/2-inch-thick, round "biscuits". Set on a greased cookie sheet. Bake 30 minutes, or until biscuits are slightly browned. Cool 30 minutes before serving.

> How You Can Make Your Own Pet Food
> www.make-stuff.com/cooking/petfood.html
> Easy instructions for dogs, cats and even budgies.

Heal your pets holistically

If you believe herbs might be good for your health, why shouldn't your pets get the same natural treatment? Here are some suggestions.

> **Herbs for Pets**
> www.naturalark.com/herbpet.html
> **Specific herbs for specific disorders.**

POPULATION

Don't speak to me of shortage. My world is vast
And has more than enough—for no more than enough.
There is a shortage of nothing, save will and wisdom
But there is a longage of people.
—Garrett Hardin (1975)

There are currently more than six billion people on the planet. It is estimated that the world could probably naturally support two to three billion people at the most. The fact that more are currently alive is a tribute to cheap oil, which has "pushed" the planet's capabilities in order to produce enough food to feed (most of) those people.

When a population of animals or plants grows beyond its optimal size, nature has ways of bringing that population down to its appropriate size. These measures include predators, disease and natural catastrophes (catastrophic from the *population's* point-of-view; Nature may feel otherwise). There is no scientific or historical reason that a human population should be an exception.

Use birth control

Yes, birth control measures do work. If used. With birth control, there is no reason for an unwanted—and certainly not an unexpected—child. Have a child only if you want one. Avoid the trauma of unwanted pregnancy, abortion, or an unwanted baby.

> **Planned Parenthood**
> **www.plannedparenthood.org**
> **Information on health care, parenthood and birth control.**

Adopt

Tragically, there *are* spare children in the world. If you want a child, there are ways to lovingly raise a child without actually bringing a new human into an over-crowded world. Check with your local social service agencies for information on how to start the adoption process.

> **Child Welfare Information Gateway**
> **www.childwelfare.gov/adoption**
> **Resources on all aspects of domestic and intercountry adoption. From the U.S. Dept. of Health and Human Services.**

Have only one child

This is a hard one, but very important. The current population of China is about 1.3 billion people. It is estimated that if China had not instituted the policy of "one child per family" thirty years ago, the country's current population would be 300 million larger.

Birth control, and self-limiting the size of families, is the only way that the planet's population can be *safely* reduced. (As mentioned above, Nature has, if needed, other ways to deal with an overpopulation problem.)

Shared housing, such as cohousing (page 34), is just one of the ways that your single child can still have plenty of opportunity to play, socialize and bond with other children. You don't have to supply all of his/her playmates yourself.

World Population Awareness
www.overpopulation.org
Goal is to preserve the environment and its natural resources for the benefit of people, families, and future generations.

Dieoff
www.dieoff.org
A grim look at the future.

Sierra Club
www.sierraclub.org/population
Global population and the environment.

Tragedy of the Commons
http://en.wikipedia.org/wiki/Tragedy_of_the_commons
Wikipedia article.

Population Connection
www.populationconnection.org
Formerly *Zero Population Growth*.

Neighborhood

ORGANIZE AND SHARE

It's good to have a home that's self-sufficient but even better to have an entire neighborhood that can cover its own basic needs. Plus your neighbors are likely to have knowledge, skills and tools that you don't have. Through mutual sharing, you're all strengthened.

The first step is to determine what your neighborhood is. In an urban area, it might be one block of a street or your apartment building. In the rural countryside, a much larger area. In a suburb, it might be several blocks, a large cul-de-sac, or a cluster of units in a condominium complex. It probably comes down to what you and your immediate neighbors feel is your neighborhood. And keep in mind that the boundaries you originally determine may change as you begin to organize.

Organize your neighborhood

To get through hard times, you need a support group that's bigger than just your family. That's where neighborhoods come in, or even an entire community if it's small enough.

Neighborhood cooperation allows all of you to speak in one voice to local government, whether it's city or county, making sure that your needs, interests, and opinions are respected.

You can begin to organize your neighborhood by talking to people you already know, and introducing yourself to others. Then hold a meeting at your home, or at a local school, place of worship, or other community-focused building.

Neighbors can discuss sharing tools, planting a neighborhood garden, and ensuring food and water supplies. If there are elderly and disabled in your area, you can discuss how best to look after them in any future event. Once your neighborhood starts to get organized, contact other neighborhoods and work with them to lobby elected officials, government agencies, public utilities, and the like, to make sure they're doing everything they can to assist your entire community in becoming as self-sufficient as possible.

Hold a neighborhood meeting. Make it comfortable and informal, with snacks and light beverages. Schedule regular meetings thereafter. Make at least every second or third meeting a social event as well as a planning one, so that people can socialize and get to know each other. Be sure to include teenagers and older children who wish to get involved.

- Make and distribute a list of everyone's name, address, phone number, fax number and email address.
- Set up a "phone tree" (a list of designated phone numbers for people to call) to notify neighbors about meetings, events and other timely information. The "phone" tree can be telephone, email, or both.
- Identify the elderly, disabled, and others needing special care and attention.

+ Create a Skills Inventory for members of your neighborhood (medical, first aid, alternative healing, midwifery, ham radio, teaching, carpentry, electrical, sewing, plumbing, music, firearms, mechanic, welding, computer, gardening, cooking, canning, childcare, etc.). This will result from occupations, hobbies, interests and other sources. People may be surprised just how many skills they have as a group once they go through this process.

+ Create a Resource Inventory of "things" owned by people in the neighborhood that they are willing to share. There is an incredible amount of duplication of expenses within a neighborhood. Garden equipment, specialty kitchen equipment (like canning tools), automotive repair tools, power tools, wells and other water sources, firewood, barbeques, generators, fuel, chain saws, amateur radio, and CB radios. Most of these are not items you need every day, but rather only for special occasions. Not every household needs to have a complete set of all this equipment.

+ Keep in mind that since you now have an entire neighborhood organized, your purchasing leverage has increased. You should be able to negotiate group discounts and bulk purchases, since many of your fellow neighbors will be wanting to purchase the same things. That's just one of the many advantages of organizing your neighborhood.

+ Use your neighborhood organization to lobby for your needs with local government. Coordinate with the city and other neighborhoods to make sure the needs of the entire community are served.

Carpool and share errand trips

Check with neighbors to see if you can start a carpool to work, or even just for errands around town or to a neighboring city. It's possible also to do errands for neighbors and have them return the favor for you at another time. You'll all save on time and gasoline money.

Start a neighborhood garden

(See page 85.)

Share tools and equipment

Once you've done your Resource Inventory, you can set up a system for sharing. It might be a central location with some sort of checkout procedure, or simply a list of who has what that they're willing to share.

Transform neighborhood schools into neighborhood centers

If there's room, set aside a space in a school for retired neighbors to meet, play cards and enjoy other pastimes. In the evenings hold neighborhood and club meetings, show films, and sponsor other events. Integrate all members of the neighborhood into the school, and all students, teachers and staff into the neighborhood. If there is no neighborhood school, try to find another public building or perhaps a church, mosque, synagogue or temple.

Start a neighborhood newsletter

Keep everyone in your neighborhood informed by starting a newsletter. You can print out copies and deliver them door-to-door, post them in central places where everyone can see them, or produce them as an email letter. Or, you can distribute newsletters using all these ways to make sure everyone has an opportunity to see them.

The newsletter can contain such information as: neighborhood projects, new tools available for sharing, neighborhood meetings, interest groups, kids' activities, classes, gardening tips. You're limited only by your resources, needs and imagination.

Here are web resources with extensive information on organizing your neighborhood and bringing its members together in a stronger neighborhood community.

Center for Neighborhood Technology
www.cnt.org

Chicago-based organization showing urban communities locally and across the country how to develop more sustainably.

Neighborhood Association Manual
www.cityofsalem.net/export/departments/neighbor/manual.htm

Designed by Salem, Oregon for the city's neighborhood association chairpersons, but an excellent model for any community.

Neighborhoods Online
www.neighborhoodsonline.net

Resource center for people working to build strong communities throughout the United States. From the Institute for the Study of Civic Values and Philadelphia's LibertyNet.

Organizing for Neighborhood Development
www.tenant.net/Organize/orgdev.html

A handbook for citizen groups.

Seattle, Washington - Department of Neighborhoods
www.seattle.gov/neighborhoods

Pioneer in the United States in organizing and supporting neighborhoods.

Great Meetings
www.cityofseattle.net/neighborhoods/pubs/meets.pdf

How to prepare for a great neighborhood meeting [pdf].

Neighborhood Organizing
www.cityofseattle.net/neighborhoods/nmf/booklets/
Neighborhood Organizing word doc.pdf

Examples of several different types of successful neighborhood self-help organizations including ad-hoc project groups, a baby-sitting co-op, an "empowerment" group, and a "community building" group. Also addresses the issues of whether to hire staff, how to raise and manage money, organizational structure, membership recruitment, and organizational self-evaluation.

The Secrets of Membership Recruitment
www.cityofseattle.net/neighborhoods/pubs/secrets.pdf

Proven tips for recruiting organization members [pdf].

Superbia [book]
Author: Dan Chiras

31 ways to create sustainable neighborhoods.

Suburban Living

The suburbs created in the United States—and, unfortunately, elsewhere—over the past 50 years could only have happened with widespread use of the private automobile, fueled by the cheap gasoline that resulted from cheap oil.

Few suburban tract home developments have stores, services, schools and employment within walking distance. Almost all require automobiles to get their inhabitants to and from their destinations. Those destinations are generally surrounded by vast areas of asphalt, that provide a daytime resting place for the cars that brought their humans to shop and work.

With its winding maze of streets and *cul de sacs*, the world of suburbia offers little to the pedestrian who actually wants to go somewhere, rather than simply walk around out front. Since the invention of the automatic door opener, neighbors have seen even less of each other as they drive into the garage, lower their door and enter their domicile, not to be seen until the garage doors automatically open in the morning, spewing their residents back onto the streets for yet another daily ritual.

The suburbs are a great place to be if you're a car; their value to humans is questionable, particularly if those humans are forced to go on foot because of high gas prices.

James Howard Kunstler, author of "The Geography of Nowhere - The Rise and Decline of America's Man-Made Landscape" and "The Long Emergency", calls the creation of suburbia "the greatest misallocation of resources in the history of the world".

Can suburbia be saved? The most pessimistic see its future as a wasteland, the slums of the future where empty buildings are cannibalized for their resources, and streets become impassable from lack of repair. Those who are more hopeful see suburbia transformed into a world of small villages, where the former residence-only streets are filled not only with homes—now with their own vegetable gardens—but also with shops, entertainment, small neighborhood schools, community meeting places, light industry and offices. All this with far less asphalt and much more green. In short, places where people live, work and play, all within walking distance.

But to get to this more optimistic future, many changes have to be made. If you live in such a neighborhood, here are some things you can do to make your neighborhood more sustainable and people-friendly.

Change zoning to mixed use

Lobby your city council and planning commission to get them to do the following things:

- Eliminate almost all single-use zoning and change it to mixed-use zoning. Let people convert homes scattered throughout the area into mom-and-pop stores, services and restaurants. Owners will be able to live in, above, or next door, to their businesses; customers will be able to walk from their homes to the businesses.
- Convert some buildings in office parks into apartments and condominiums. Turn some of the offices into businesses serving the residents of those apartments and condominiums.
- Revitalize downtown areas of towns and cities by building new apartments right in the downtown area. Convert buildings, add a story of residential space above existing businesses, tear down old buildings and erect new ones for housing.
- Put living units in shopping malls. Set up telecommuting centers in the malls. Use some of that vast parking area to construct new apartment buildings. Rip up some of the asphalt for gardens.
- Encourage people to work from their homes, and provide tax advantages for those who do.

Run paths through *cul de sacs*

Get your city to put paths and trails connecting *cul de sacs* with the *cul de sacs* and streets behind them, so that people can walk easily from one location to another without having to wander along an endless maze of sidewalks to get to what is actually a close destination.

If the city won't do it, figure out a way you and your neighbors can make it happen yourselves.

Take down the fences

Take down your back and side fences and open up the area behind your home. As other neighbors do this, a beautiful parkland can be created. You'll have a private, community park for the use of residents on the block. Kids can play safely, vegetable gardens can be planted, and the feeling of community and neighborliness will be enhanced.

"N" Street Cohousing in Davis, California is a cohousing (page 34) group that was started in 1986 when two tract homes built in the early 1950s took down their side fences. "N" Street continues to grow slowly, adding one house at a time. Currently they've expanded to 17 houses, 10 homes on "N" Street that back up to 7 homes on the adjacent street. (Two of the homes on N Street are across the street from the community but are active members.)

The removal of fences has created a beautiful open-space area that includes vegetable, flower, and water gardens; a play structure; a hot tub; a sauna; and a chicken coop, large grassy area, pond and more.

N Street Cohousing
www.nstreetcohousing.org
The Davis cohousing community's website.

Convert lawns into gardens

(See page 32.)

Superbia [book]
Author: Dan Chiras
31 Ways to Create Sustainable Neighborhoods.

Suburban Nation [book]
Author: Andre Duany

The Rise of Sprawl and the Decline of the American
Dream.

The Geography of Nowhere [book]
Author: James Howard Kunstler
The Rise and Decline of America's Man-Made Landscape.

The Long Emergency
Author: James Howard Kunstler

Surviving the Converging Catastrophes of the Twenty-
First Century.

Community

Community is an abstract term and often more a feeling than a place with rigid, geographic limits. Your community is the area that you feel most connected with, though it's probably bigger than just your neighborhood. In most cases it will be your entire town, although in a large metropolitan city, it could simply be the district in which you live.

Sustainable living works best at the community level, where people work—and play—together.

The first step, as we said earlier, is to organize your neighborhood (page 46).

Another is to open, or support, a "Third Place", preferably in each neighborhood, but certainly in several locations throughout the community.

Third Places

Sociologist Ray Oldenburg, author of *The Great Good Place*, has coined the term "third place" for the places where community members informally hang out to socialize, discuss business deals, and talk about their lives and their community. The first place is home, the second is work. Third places are not private clubs, but locations where anyone in the community can drop by, have a cup of coffee or a beer, say hello to friends and join in on a conversation.

Third Places are disappearing everywhere as small, local businesses have a harder and harder time competing with chains (such as Starbuck's, which considers itself a third place), and as local taverns, corner stores and bookstores disappear from the scene.

A community with no third places is no community. If you don't have enough of them, start one. Start one downtown, or even in your neighborhood. In fact, every neighborhood or district in town should have at least one.

For an example, check out Third Place Commons (www.thirdplacecommons.org) in the Seattle area, which was actually created as a third place, rather than being one that evolved over the years.

> **Celebrating the Third Place [book]**
> **Editor: Ray Oldenburg**
>
> **Inspiring Stories About the "Great Good Places" at the Heart of Our Communities.**
>
> **The Great Good Place [book]**
> **Author: Ray Oldenburg**
>
> **Cafés, Coffee Shops, Bookstores, Bars, Hair Salons, and Other Hangouts at the Heart of a Community. Oldenburg's original book.**

"Think locally, act locally" (but communicate *globally*)

Sustainability really means making your community self-sufficient, or at least as self-sufficient as possible. But solutions—and failures—that your community encounters can be communicated to other communities around the country and around the world. By communicating globally—primarily on the Internet—we can all share these ideas, successes and failures. Don't keep your community's actions a secret. Let those in other communities know what you've learned—what worked and what didn't.

LOCAL BUSINESS

Locally owned businesses help the local economy. Chain stores don't.

A study done in the Andersonville neighborhood of Chicago found:

- Local merchants generate substantially greater economic impact than chain retailers.
- Development of urban sites with directly competitive chain merchants will reduce the overall vigor of the local economy.
- Modest changes in consumer spending habits can generate substantial local economic impact.
- For every $100 in consumer spending with a local firm, $68 remains in the Chicago economy vs. $43 for spending at a chain store.
- For every square foot occupied by a local firm, local economic impact is $179 vs. $105 for a chain store

Shop at locally owned businesses

Buy everything, including food, from locally-owned businesses. Even better, whenever possible buy not just from local businesses but from local *producers* (farmers, craftsmen, manufacturers).

The more food, goods and services that are produced within your community, the more you can depend on those things continuing to be produced. Because they will require little or no transport, they will be much less dependent on oil supplies, except for that needed in their production.

The people who own and work at those businesses are your friends, neighbors and fellow members of your community. They have the same stake in the community's success and health as do you. They're much more inclined to donate to local youth groups, schools and non-profit organizations than are chain stores. And the money they make is much more inclined to remain in the community, supporting other businesses, than is money that goes into the chain store vacuum to end up in a distant city.

If you own a business, it's particularly important that you use local and locally owned vendors, producers and manufacturers. Local businesses should support each other for the same reason that local customers should support local businesses. If you don't buy locally, why should you expect the residents of your community to buy from you?

> **Relocalization Network**
> **www.relocalize.net**
>
> **Support for Post Carbon Institute's Local Post Carbon Groups to increase community energy security, strengthen local economies, and dramatically improve environmental conditions and social equity.**

If you own a business, join with other locally owned businesses

BALLE (the Business Alliance for Local Living Economies) and AMIBA (American Independent Business Alliance) are two national organizations that have local chapters supporting local business communities. You can help them spread their message of local economic independence, and they'll help you and your community's business interests. Check with them to see if there's already a chapter in your community. If not, start one.

Business Alliance for Local Living Economies (BALLE)
165-11th Street
San Francisco, CA 94103
415.255.1108
www.livingeconomies.org

Building long-term economic empowerment and prosperity in communities through local business ownership, economic justice, cultural diversity and a healthy natural environment.

American Independent Business Alliance (AMIBA)
222 South Black Ave.
Bozeman, MT 59715
406.582.1255
www.amiba.net

Locally owned independent businesses, citizens and community organizations united to support home town business.

Andersonville Study of Retail Economics
www.andersonvillestudy.com

The study quoted at the beginning of this section.

Benefits of Doing Business Locally
http://reclaimdemocracy.org/independent_business/local_business_benefits.html

Benefits to communities and citizens in patronizing local businesses.

Buying Local and the Circulating Dollar
www.blueoregon.com/2005/11/buying_local_an.html

Often local business prices are lower than chain stores, and the money you spend there stays in the community.

Local Ownership Pays Off for Communities
www.reclaimdemocracy.org/independent_business/local_ownership_pays.html

Financial benefits to the community of locally owned businesses.

> **The Home Town Advantage**
> www.newrules.org/retail
>
> **Reviving locally owned business - From the New Rules Project.**

LOCAL CURRENCY

Money is the central focus of our society and it's extremely difficult to get away from that focus. Some try to work with money in ways that benefit a community rather than just individuals. Networks supporting locally owned businesses (page 59) are one of these ways; "community currencies" are another.

Many people have no faith in the government's currency since it can be printed by the government in quantities with no apparent limitations, and has no real backing in reality. It is "faith-based".

Local Currency, also called Community Currency, is paper currency printed and distributed locally, of value only within a community. (Note: New systems are being used which use *digital* local currency instead of paper only.) This currency remains in the community instead of being removed by distant owners. It circulates from person to person, business to business, benefiting the entire community.

Local currency can also empower citizens who may not normally be involved in the economic life of their community. And it's popular when no one trusts the national currency, as was seen throughout the United States and other countries during the Great Depression of the 1930s.

If you were in the U.S. military in Vietnam, you used local currency. There it was called "Military Payment Certificate (MPC)", usable only at U.S. installations. If you've ever been to a Disney theme park, you probably used "Disney Dollars". That's also local currency, although it benefits a corporation and not a community. (A rumored 60% of the currency is kept as souvenirs and never spent, resulting in nice profits to Disney just for printing paper.)

Local currency, which usually involves use of locally printed money (yes, it's legal) but may also be done with digital credits, is often confused with *barter*, which involves only goods and services and no currency. We recommend you also look into barter (page 139), which quite nicely complements the use of local currency.

If there is no local currency system, start one

Talk to small, locally owned businesses, particularly health food stores, bookstores, farmers markets, and cooperative stores. Many of these businesses already appreciate the value of community and cooperation. A locally owned bank may also understand the value of local currency.

Gather a small group together and start small, expanding as you feel more comfortable with the system.

Complementary Currency Resource Center
www.complementarycurrency.org

Information, resources, step-by-step instructions, online assistance, and forums.

Starter Local Currency Kit for your community
www.lightlink.com/hours/ithacahours/starterkit.html

Hometown money book and samples of money.

Whenever there's a choice, patronize a business that accepts local currency

Patronizing businesses that accept local currency supports those businesses and encourages them to continue their policy. Let other businesses know you'll patronize them also, once they start accepting the currency.

If you have a business or skill, make it available to the public using local currency

Local currency provides an excellent way for individuals to integrate into the local economy. Your individual services can be listed in the local currency members directory right along with established businesses in town.

Community Currencies
www.transaction.net/money/cc/cc01.html

How local currency can help solve the problems of unemployment, the environment, and community breakdown. The philosophy, history and potential for the 21st century.

Complementary Currencies
www.transaction.net/money/community/

Extensive information and resources on complementary community currency systems and local exchange networks.

E.F. Schumacher Society Home Page
www.schumachersociety.org

Linking people, land, and community by building local economies. Named after the author of *Small Is Beautiful: Economics As If People Mattered.*

E.F.Schumacher Society's Local Currency Page
www.smallisbeautiful.org/local_currencies.html

Fair Trade
www.newdream.org/newsletter/fairtrade.php

On community currency and other systems.

Grassroots Economics
www.context.org/ICLIB/IC41/Glover.htm

Local currency in Ithaca, New York.

Ithaca HOURS
www.ithacahours.org

Detailed information on the Ithaca community currency.

Ithaca HOURS Online
www.lightlink.com/hours/ithacahours

Locally issued paper money from a well established community currency project in Ithaca, New York.

LETSystems
www.gmlets.u-net.com

Lets (Local Employment Trading System) is a trading network supported by its own internal currency. It is self-regulating and allows its users to manage and issue their own "money supply" within the boundaries of the network.

Barter/LETS 101
www.cyberclass.net/bartable.htm

Usury-free software information for LETS and LETS communities around the world.

Let's Go Global with Barter
www.alternatives.ca/article138.html

But actually about LETS.

More on LETS
www.transaction.net/money/lets/

From Transaction.net ncluding links to communities using the system.

> **Self-sufficiency Economy by Own Money**
> www.appropriateeconomics.org/asia/thailand/
> self_sufficiency_economy.htm
> Community barter [currency] system in a Thai village.
>
> **Time Dollar**
> www.timebanks.org
> A time-based currency where one hour spent helping
> another earns one Time Dollar.

SPREAD THE WORD

Sustainability works best when many people practice it, supporting and encouraging each other. Let others in your community know what you're doing.

Start a community newspaper

It would be simpler if your local newspaper(s) covered the issues of sustainable living. If no local paper does—or will—see if *you* can write a weekly column in a paper on sustainable living and neighborhood/community actions. If the local paper isn't interested even in a column, consider starting your own paper, even if it's published only once or twice a month. Remember, though, that it's a huge effort and you'll likely need the help of others to make it happen.

Start a local radio station

Currently, in the United States, it's very difficult to get permission from the federal government to start a full-power radio station. In the meantime, consider a low-power AM or FM station. It will probably have enough power to cover at least your neighborhood. And a number of low-power stations can be linked up to cover the entire community.

> **Prometheus Radio Project**
> www.prometheusradio.org
>
> Non-profit organization supporting low power community radio stations.
>
> **Low Power FM**
> www.lpfm.ws
>
> Information on legal low-power FM stations in the United States.
>
> **Low Power AM**
> www.lpam.info
>
> Lots of information and a free Low Power AM Broadcasters Handbook.

If that's not workable, consider an Internet radio station, using either streaming audio or podcasting. Streaming audio lets people click on a website and listen to music, discussion, news or other content. Podcasting allows them to download the audio content to their iPod or other mp3 player in order to listen to programs whenever and wherever they wish.

> **Internet Radio**
> http://en.wikipedia.org/wiki/Internet_radio
> From Wikipedia.

Starting an Internet Radio Station
www.allinternetradio.com/stationguide.asp

Step-by-step instructions.

How to Start an Internet Radio Station
http://music.lovetoknow.com/
How_To_Start_An_Internet_Radio_Station

Instructions and links to resources.

Podcasting
http://en.wikipedia.org/wiki/Podcasting

From Wikipedia.

How to Podcast
www.how-to-podcast-tutorial.com

Step-by-step guide.

A Pattern Language: Towns, Buildings, Construction
[book]
Author: Christopher Alexander

Architect Christopher Alexander's almost legendary opus
on the elements that make a building or an entire town
truly human.

Pattern Language
www.patternlanguage.com

Alexander's website is also highly recommended. You'll
find lots of information and resources.

Citizens Handbook
www.vcn.bc.ca/citizens-handbook
A guide to building community. Highly recommended.

Community Collaboration
www.communitycollaboration.net
Helping communities and organizations build
collaboration and consensus.

Community Solution
www.communitysolution.org

Dedicated to the development, growth and enhancement of small local communities.

Toward Sustainable Communities [book]
Author: Mark Roseland

Resources for Citizens and Their Governments.

Utopian EcoVillage Network
www.uevn.org

U.S. organization dedicated to the development, growth and enhancement of small local communities with a focus on dealing with Peak Oil.

Going Local [book]
Author: Michael Shuman
Creating self-reliant communities in a global age.

Local Government Commission (LGC)
www.lgc.org

Working to build livable communities.

Center for Livable Communities
www.lgc.org/center

From the Local Government Commission. Extensive information and resources.

The Natural Step for Communities [book]
Author: Sarah James

How cities and towns can change to sustainable practices.

Partners for Livable Communities
www.livable.com

Working to improve the livability of communities by promoting quality of life, economic development, and social equity.

Stop Sprawl
www.sierraclub.org/sprawl/community
Sierra Club on livable communities. Lots of information
and resources.

Community Energy Opportunity Finder
www.energyfinder.org

An interactive tool that will help you determine your
community's best bets for energy solutions that benefit
the local economy, the community, and the environment.
Developed by Rocky Mountain Institute.

Bowling Alone
www.bowlingalone.com

Based on Robert Putnam's book on declining social
capital.

Better Together
www.bettertogether.org
Tools and strategies to connect with others.

INTENTIONAL COMMUNITIES / ECOVILLAGES

It takes a village to raise an adult. We all need villages, even if
they're just mini-villages in urban areas. (We call those
"neighborhoods".) Many people around the planet are
working together to create new, or modify old, communities
to be sustainable, to focus on humans not cars, and to provide
healthy, people-friendly places to work, play, grow and learn.

While the focus of this book is to help you live a more sustainable life where you are now, you might be interested in learning more about communities specifically designed to be sustainable.

City Comforts [book]
Author: David Sucher

How to build an urban village.

Communities Directory [book]
Editor: Fellowship of Intentional Communities

A guide to intentional communities and cooperative living.

Creating a Life Together [book]
Author: Diana Leafe Christian

Practical Tools to Grow Ecovillages and Intentional Communities.

Ecovillage Living [book]
Author: Hildur Jackson

Restoring the Earth and Her People.

Ecovillages [book]
Author: Jan Martin Bang

A practical guide to sustainable communities.

Global Ecovillage Network
www.ecovillages.org

A global confederation of people and communities, both urban and rural, that meet and share ideas, exchange technologies, and develop cultural and educational exchanges, directories and newsletters. An outstanding resource

Intentional Communities
www.ic.org

A worldwide guide to ecovillages, cohousing, residential land trusts, communes, student co-ops, urban housing cooperatives and other related projects and dreams.

GET INVOLVED

Despite what many people think, democracy was not intended to be a spectator sport. It's not simply reading about government in the paper, watching it on TV, or gossiping about Hollywood stars' latest political advocacy. It also wasn't intended to be democracy-for-hire, where we send political mercenaries a check and they do what we ask them to do.

Democracy is a *participatory* activity, or it is nothing at all. That means you get out and participate. Organize your neighborhood to accomplish neighborhood projects and to make its voice heard at city hall.

Your first step, as we've stated before, is to organize your neighborhood (page 46). That's the level where democracy truly begins. Your neighborhood is not just your closest mini-community, it's one of the building blocks of the entire community. If your neighborhood is organized, you can represent the many voices—and votes—of your neighborhood at the community level. You can get city help to accomplish neighborhood projects, and to give the residents of your neighborhood a combined voice at city hall.

Community level actions

Represent your neighborhood at city hall. Join with other neighborhoods to participate in neighborhood-based city government. Volunteer for a community group. Run for school board or city council. Start a city-wide organization for a particular cause that needs to be addressed. Join or start groups to influence local policy. Run for local office or apply for appointed positions on committees and commissions. Work with others to discuss and deal with local problems and needs.

Other neighborhoods

If you find that you've done everything you can for your own home and neighborhood, branch out. Take your skills and expertise to another neighborhood and see if there are ways you can assist its residents. Or check with your city government to see if they can suggest other areas where you can help.

Remember also that your community has many groups that are already organized and in place. These include religious congregations, service clubs, women's clubs, youth groups, business groups, and the like. Coordinate with them to help their members and the community as a whole implement as many of the suggestions in this book as appropriate.

City/county government

If you're involved with local government as an elected or appointed official, or a member of city or county staff, you're in a position to help make some important changes. We suggest the following as three of the most important of those changes.

Change zoning to mixed use

Allow—and even demand—housing in commercial and light-industrial areas, and commercial in residential areas.

One of the great tragedies of suburban city planning since World War II has been the ghettoization of zoning. Housing is not allowed in commercial areas; commercial uses are not allowed in residential areas. The result has been that people are forced to drive from one area to take advantage of the benefits located in the other area. Your community is more sustainable when the zoning encourages walking and discourages driving.

For example, few people in tract housing areas are within walking distance of grocery stores, dry cleaners, retail shops and all the other commercial services we need on a regular basis. So they, and their children, are forced to travel by car to these destinations. Fossil fuels are wasted, money is wasted, and health deteriorates due to lack of opportunity to walk. Ideally a home should never be more than a five or ten minute walk from all these shops and services—one planning concept that is supported in most urban areas.

Enforce and support water and energy conservation

Encourage and, if necessary, demand cuts in water and energy use. In support, set up a municipal plan that subsidizes such things as low-flow toilets and the replacement of incandescent bulbs with compact fluorescent bulbs.

Establish and support local power generation

Depending on the environmental conditions, strive to generate at least some of your community's electrical power through sustainable local sources, for example wind, hydro, solar, or tidal. This could involve financially and technically assisting homes and neighborhoods, or even building municipal power plants or "energy farms".

Food

GARDENING

Growing your own food is essential to improving your self-sufficiency. No matter how much food you're able to grow, it all helps. The more you grow, the less you have to buy at the store.

When you grow your own food, you know exactly how it has been grown. If you wish, you can grow organically, using non-hybrid "heirloom" seeds, assuring that you get the healthiest, tastiest and most nutritious food possible.

No matter how small your living space, you can still grow some of your own food, even if it's just sprouts (page 95), herbs, or a couple of tomato plants.

Start a home garden

A garden in your yard can be as small or large as you wish and have space for. A 4'x4' area can produce a lot of food, particularly if you do "intensive" gardening.

There are many different methods, styles, techniques, and theories of gardening. We suggest you visit your local nursery and ask their advice. They know the soil and climate in your area. You can also check with your local gardening clubs or, if you live in the United States, your local agricultural advisor or Master Gardeners branch.

The basic steps of gardening are always the same: find a location, prepare the soil, plant seeds or seedlings, care for the plants, and harvest.

Here are the steps you'll follow if you use the popular Square Foot Gardening techniques recommended by Mel Bartholomew.

- Location – pick a site that has six to eight hours of sun a day
- Layout – arrange your garden in squares, not rows
- Boxes – build boxes to hold soil mix
- Aisles – space boxes three feet apart
- Soil – fill boxes with soil mix
- Grid – make a grid for the top of each box
- Care – never walk on the soil
- Select – determine a different crop for each square foot
- Plant – conserve seeds, planting only two or three seeds per hole
- Water – water by hand from a bucket
- Harvest – when each square is harvested, plant a new crop

Square Foot Gardening
www.squarefootgardening.com
"How would you like a garden filled with beautiful flowers, fresh herbs and luscious vegetables, but no weeds and no hard work?" - From the website.

Square Foot Gardening Video
Available at above website
Video and DVD versions of the popular book.

Acres U.S.A. Magazine
www.acresusa.com
A voice for eco-agriculture.

California Backyard Orchard, The
http://homeorchard.ucdavis.edu

If you've got the room, grow your own fruits and nuts.
From the University of California.

Gardening Without Irrigation
www.gutenberg.org/etext/4512

Free downloadable e-book.

Lawns to Gardens
www.yougrowgirl.com/lawns_gardens_convert.php

How to convert your lawn to your garden.

Organic Gardening
www.organic-gardening.net

Good information and resources.

Master Gardeners
www.ahs.org/master_gardeners

American Horticultural Society guide to Master Gardeners
throughout the United States. The gardeners provide free
expert advice and training to home gardeners.

National Gardening Association
www.garden.org

Very extensive information.

You Grow Girl
www.yougrowgirl.com

Practical information in a friendly gardening site.

How to Grow More Vegetables [book]
Author: John Jeavons

And fruits, nuts, berries, grains and other crops than you
ever thought possible on less land than you can imagine.

The Sustainable Vegetable Garden [book]
Author: John Jeavons

A backyard guide to healthy soil and higher yields.

Start a neighborhood or community garden

(See page 85.)

Start a hydroponic garden

Hydroponics is growing plants without soil and goes back, at least, to the Hanging Gardens of Babylon. Your hydroponic garden doesn't have to be as elaborate as the one in Babylon, but you can still produce tasty vegetables, fruits and herbs. You can also grow them inside an apartment year-round because you don't even need natural sunlight.

Studies have shown that hydroponically-grown food can be as much as 50% higher in nutrients and vitamins than field-grown food.

It's easiest if you use a kit to get started. It can cost $100 and up, but of course it's reusable again and again.

Homegrown Hydroponics
www.hydroponics.com/info
Very comprehensive site on all aspects of hydroponics.

Hydroponics Mailing List
Hydroponics.org
Mailing list for discussion about hydroponics, growing methods, tools, supplies, and more.

Simply Hydro
www.simplyhydro.com
Hydroponics and organics, including the free online "Hydro U." classes.

Garden using biodynamics

Biodynamics is an agriculture system initiated by philosopher/scientist Rudolf Steiner in the 1920s. More than just organic, it seeks to work with and revitalize the life forces in the plants and soil, and with the seasonal cycles of nature.

Biodynamic and Organic Gardening
www.biodynamic.net

Excellent source of links and books.

Biodynamic Farming and Compost Preparation
http://attra.ncat.org/attra-pub/biodynamic.html

Extensive information from the National Sustainable
Agriculture Information Service.

Biodynamics
www.biodynamics.com

Biodynamic Farming and Gardening Association.

What is Biodynamics?
www.biodynamics.net.au/what_is_biodynamics.htm

From Biodynamic Agriculture Australia.

What is Biodynamics?
www.biodynamics.com/biodynamics.html

A philosophical view.

Garden using permaculture

Permaculture was created in the 1970s by two Australian
ecologists, Bill Mollison and David Holmgren. They developed
an ever-changing and expanding system of agriculture that
has evolved over the years. It is a philosophy of ethics,
personal responsibility and balanced ecology working with,
rather than against, the natural world to create sustainable
human habitats.

Permaculture farming is now done all over the world, on
both large and small-scale sites. Permaculture has evolved into
far more than just gardening or farming, but those aspects of it
are a good place to start.

Crystal Waters
www.crystalwaters.org.au
Permaculture village in Australia.

Gaia's Garden [book]
Author:Toby Hemenway
A guide to home-scale Permaculture.

Global Gardener
Video on Permaculture by co-founder Bill Mollison
[video].

Introduction to Permaculture [book]
Author: Bill Mollison
By the man who started the Permaculture movement.

Permaculture
http://en.wikipedia.org/wiki/Permaculture
From Wikipedia.

Permaculture [book]
Author: David Holmgren
Principles and pathways beyond sustainability by the co-founder of Permaculture.

Permaculture Institute
www.permaculture.org
Promotion and support of the sustainability of human culture and settlements.

Permaculture Resources
www.permacultureactivist.net
Good selection of articles, books and videos.

Tagari Publications
www.tagari.com
Publishes and distributes the best in Permaculture research. Established by Permaculture founder Bill Mollison.

> Urban Permaculture Guild
> www.urbanpermacultureguild.org
> Group action to help transform urban places.
>
> Permaculture in a Nutshell [book]
> Author: Patrick Whitefield
> An introduction to permaculture.

Remineralize your soil

Remineralization revitalizes soils by imitating natural processes and using materials ("rock dust") that are a result of glaciation, volcanic eruptions, and alluvial deposits to restore the soil with its natural nutrients. Remineralization provides slow, natural release of elements and trace minerals, rebalances soil pH, increases resistance to insects and disease, and produces larger and more nutritious crops.

You can find "rock dust" for little or no cost (at local quarries, for example), add it to your garden, and see the results for yourself.

> On a Fad Diet of Rock Dust, How Does the Garden Grow?
> www.gardening-guy.com/stories/storyReader$37
> Article from *New York Time*.
>
> Remineralize the Earth
> Remineralize.org
> Non-profit organization incorporated to disseminate ideas and practice about soil remineralization throughout the world. Site offers two free ebooks on soil mineralization.
>
> Rock Dust Grows Extra-Big Vegetables (and Might Save Us from Global Warming)
> www.commondreams.org/headlines05/0321-02.htm
> Article from *The Independent*.

Use heirloom seeds

Western society (at least in the United States) has gone from eating hundreds, if not thousands, of different varieties of vegetables, to the few, standard vegetables found at most dinner tables. The choice is limited because most of our food is grown on large, corporate-owned and monocultural farms. Such a farm would grow, for example, only one or at the most two types of tomatoes, all hybrids designed for high-yield and the ability to be tough enough to fight off disease and travel long distances. Taste and nutrition are not at the top of the corporate goals.

"Heirloom" (non-hybrid vegetables popular before the industrialization of agriculture) seed companies and organizations seek to preserve the original biodiversity, and promote sustainable, organic agriculture with traditional, vegetable, flower and herb seeds, all organic, non-hybrid, and non-genetically modified. Why? Because the foods produced are healthier and tastier. (Have you experienced the difference in taste between an organic heirloom tomato and a long-traveled supermarket tomato?) In the long-run, heirloom produce is more likely to survive and thrive in a changing environment than hybrids.

Organic Seed Alliance
www.seedalliance.org
Supporting the ethical stewardship and development of seed.

Seeds of Change
www.seedsofchange.com
Organic seeds, products and information.

Use vermiculture

Worms are your friends. Vermiculture, also called vermicomposting or simply "worm composting", is using earthworms to break down organic matter into nutrient-rich, natural fertilizer and soil conditioner. The worms will work 24 hours a day making compost for your garden.

You can buy earthworms online or from local sources such as fishing shops where they are sold as bait. For home use, people generally use small plastic, cardboard or wood bins, which you can buy, or build or recycle yourself for a few dollars. The only other materials you'll need are soil, old newspapers and kitchen scraps.

Composting with Red Wiggler Worms
www.cityfarmer.org/wormcomp61.html
Urban agriculture notes from City Farmer.

Vermicompost
http://en.wikipedia.org/wiki/Vermiculture
Good information from Wikipedia.

Vermiculture Resources
www.empnet.com/worms/resource.htm
Good list of links.

Vermiculture Systems
www.composters.com/docs/worms.html
Buy a worm condo for your home.

Worm Digest
www.wormdigest.org
The definitive vermiculture magazine.

Worm Poop
www.wormpoop.com
Information and products.

COMPOST

Composting your yard trimmings and kitchen waste provides a nutrient-filled addition to the soil for your lawn and garden.

Composting - A Simple Guide To Doing It
Thanks to the *Connecticut Fund for the Environment*

♦ Find a place. A corner of the yard will do. Or use a large garbage pail with holes drilled in the bottom for drainage. A wooden crate or a circular tube of chicken wire fence also works fine. Some people use trash barrels buried underground so the lid is level with the ground.

♦ Start the compost pile with a six-inch layer of dead leaves, twigs, and other yard scraps. If you can, add a one-inch layer of soil.

♦ Save food waste in a small, covered container in your kitchen. Include all of your vegetable and bread scraps, eggshells, fruit peels, coffee grounds, tea bags (with plastic tags or labels removed), pits, and seeds. Don't add beef, poultry, or fish leftovers because they attract pests. The smaller your scraps are, the faster they will decompose. Shred the material before adding it to the compost pile in order to speed up the composting process.

♦ When the kitchen container is full, dump it onto your compost pile. To make the pile more visually attractive and to enrich the pile, you can add on top leaves, grass cuttings, or weeds pulled from your garden.

- ◆ Continue to add your kitchen and yard scraps until your outdoor compost container is three-quarters full, or until the pile is three feet deep. Then leave that pile alone and let bacteria do their work to transform your food waste into a rich, dark, spongy soil.
- ◆ Follow the same directions to start a second compost container or pile. By the time your second pile is complete, the contents of the first will be ready to use as a fertilizer for your yard or garden.

Tips

To work best, the compost should be damp but not soggy. If it is too wet or too dry, the composting process will slow down. Water it when the weather is dry, and cover it during heavy rains.

A well-tended compost pile has no offensive odors. If the pile begins to give off an unpleasant odor, try covering it to keep it drier.

To speed the decomposition process, you can turn the pile every few weeks during the summer with a shovel or a pitchfork. This allows oxygen to get into the compost. If steam rises when you turn the pile, don't be alarmed. This is evidence that the composting process is at work.

Let worms help you with your compost by using vermiculture (page 82).

Learn to Compost
www.seattletilth.org/resources/compost
Extensive information on composting from Seattle Tilth.

Compost Guide
www.compostguide.com
A complete guide to making compost.

> **How to Compost**
> www.howtocompost.org
> Articles and links covering all topics about composting and organic gardening.

COMMUNITY GARDENS

Neighborhood gardens (also called "community gardens" or "urban gardens) are shared plots within an urban or neighborhood setting. Gardeners share tools, knowledge and labor to produce food for themselves and others. There are an estimated 18,000 community gardens throughout Canada and the United States.

Join a community garden

To find an existing community garden, check with your city parks department or your county or local state agricultural advisor. If that doesn't work, try the local school district. If that doesn't work, start one yourself.

Start a community garden

Talk to the city parks department or your county agricultural advisor for advice and a possible location. If that doesn't work, join up with some neighbors and search for a vacant lot or other suitable location.

If you find a location, contact the owner. You might have to go through the local planning department to find out who owns the lot. Tell the owner what you'd like to do. Tell him/her you're offering to clean up the lot for free. If that's not enough, promise the owner some of the produce you grow.

If you can't find a vacant lot, maybe you can team up with the neighborhood school. For more assistance, check with your local Master Gardeners group (in the United States) or any other local gardening club.

Here are the basic initial steps from the American Community Garden Association's document *"Starting a Community Garden"*.

1. Form a planning committee
2. Choose a site
3. Prepare and develop the site
4. Organize the garden
5. Insurance
6. Set up a new gardening organization

You'll find full details through their website listed below.

American Community Garden Association
www.communitygarden.org
Non-profit organization for rural and urban gardening.

Starting a Community Garden
www.communitygarden.org/starting.php
Free fact sheet from the ACGA.

Garden Your City [book]
Author: Barbara Hobens Feldt
How to start an urban garden.

Seattle P-Patch Community Gardens
www.seattle.gov/neighborhoods/ppatch
Pioneer in city-sponsored community gardening.

> **Seattle Tilth**
> www.seattletilth.org
>
> A leader in organic community gardens.
>
> **Master Gardeners**
> www.ahs.org/master_gardeners
>
> American Horticultural Society guide to Master
> Gardeners throughout the United States. The gardeners
> provide free expert advice and training to home
> gardeners.

Buy food from a community garden

Many community gardens donate their food to local food
banks or other organizations. They may also sell at farmers
markets. Check with the community gardens in your area to
see where they sell their food, or if you can buy vegetables
directly from them.

LOCAL FOOD

Food is so essential that we have to ensure that we have a
steady supply of it. Growing your own is the best solution.
Supporting a local farmer is also excellent, particularly since
that farmer can probably turn out a lot more, and a lot more
variety, than you can.

It makes sense to have both home and neighborhood gardens. Your home gardening can be as simple as herbs, sprouts, and a few tomatoes—or much more if you have the time and space. Community gardening benefits you by contact with your fellow neighbors as much as it does from the actual food itself.

What's the best way to grow and obtain food? That depends on you and where you live. We've tried to give you a wide variety of ideas here.

Support local farmers

Local farmers are a community treasure. Do everything you can to support them. Buy their produce at your local farmers' market. (If you don't have one, help start one.) Many local farms offers weekly delivery (or pickup) of food baskets. You can sign up for their service, paying monthly or quarterly. Community Supported Agriculture (CSA) can include paying for regular food baskets or actually investing in the farm.

Supermarket foods can travel an average of 1,200-1,500 miles before they reach your plate, using energy and resulting in increased air pollution. Buy food that is locally produced and in season, and you help reduce that energy requirement. Local farms are a valuable resource; your support helps to keep them alive. You also give yourself the pleasure—and health—of being able to eat very fresh, nutritious foods.

---

100 Mile Diet
www.100milediet.org

Join the movement. Try eating only from producers within 100 miles of your home.

Community Supported Agriculture (CSA)

CSA farms are mutually supported by individuals and families. Through ongoing contracts, farmers deliver weekly food—usually organic—to homes. In turn, the farms receive ongoing financial support.

Local Food
http://news.bbc.co.uk/2/hi/science/nature/4312591.stm
Greener than organic. BBC article.

Local Harvest
www.localharvest.org
Farmers markets, family farms, CSAs, organic food.

Robyn Van En Center
www.wilson.edu/wilson/asp/content.asp?id=804
Offers services to existing and new CSA farmers and shareholders, including a database of U.S. CSA farms.

Start a garden (home and/or community)

Whether or not you support local farms, your own garden is a must. If you have a yard, start a garden in it (replace a lawn, if necessary—see page 32). See page 74 for information on home gardens.

If you live in an apartment or condominium that doesn't have a yard, at least use containers to grow vegetables, herbs and sprouts inside your home.

Your neighborhood might want to start a larger, shared garden where many households help one another raise foods. Your community might even offer land for much larger gardens, to be shared by people from throughout the town. (See more information on Community Gardens at page 85.)

Eat organic when possible (but choose local non-organic over distantly-grown organic)

If you think the idea of organic foods is nonsense, well, then carry on. If you prefer the idea of chemical-free, pesticide-free, herbicide-free, unprocessed foods, try to get them whenever possible. Usually, they're not only chemical-free but higher in vitamins and minerals as well since the land they're grown on is almost always healthier than the soil used for mass-produced crops and livestock.

These days many of our organic foods are imported from as far away as South America or Asia. If you can buy produce from a local farmer, even if non-organic, consider if it's more worthwhile to support the efforts—and even the existence—of your local farmer than to pay for imported food that requires a large use of fossil fuels for its shipment by plane or boat.

Slow Food

Slow Food began in Italy in 1986 as a reaction to (and protest against) the primarily American fast food industry, which has contributed not only to fast, mass-produced meals but a fast, mass-produced society in most developed countries. Slow Food's manifesto states that it is a "movement for the protection of the right to taste."

Slow Food supports and encourages quality foods and beverages, and supports local growers, chefs, winemakers and others who share their goals. Slow Food USA's mission is to "rediscover pleasure and quality in everyday life precisely by slowing down and learning to appreciate the convivial traditions of the table." It does this through local chapters called "convivia" that organize educational, cultural and, most important, gastronomic events.

Slow Foods also spawned another related movement called *Slow Cities,* which also started in Italy. Slow Cities are towns under 50,000 population that have vowed to retain their local character. They focus on environmental conservation, the promotion of sustainable development, and the improvement of urban life, encouraging both residents and visitors to slow down and enjoy life.

Slow Food USA
www.slowfoodusa.org
Slow Food activities and organizations in the United States.
Slow Cities
www.cittaslow.net
Official website of the Slow City movement.

Support local markets

Just as it's important to support local farmers, it's important to support local retail food shops. Your local grocery store, greengrocer, butcher, dairy, cheese monger and the like are all locally-owned. They are members of the community and support local community activities, schools and groups. And they're more likely than chain stores to sell foods that come from the region where you live. In bad financial times, a large national supermarket chain can decide to close their store in your town; the owners of local grocery stores live in your community; they're not going anywhere.

Eat less meat

While there are health, religious, ethical, and philosophical reasons why many people don't eat meat, we suggest a very simple one. You—and society—can save money when we all cut down on meat intake. Most Americans are already getting an excess of protein. Meats can be expensive, and livestock—particularly beef cattle—consume huge quantities of feed and water in order to produce relatively small quantities of food (an estimated 2,500 gallons of water to produce one pound of beef). Much of the land that feed stock is grown on can be better used for growing vegetables and other products.

Rainforests are being destroyed in most areas to provide land for agriculture. Most of this cleared land is being used to raise cattle. And those cattle become the fast-food hamburgers of America. Because of the large number of acres of grazing land required to raise cattle, it has been estimated that every fast-food hamburger you *don't* eat will save 55 square feet of rainforest.

The meat produced in the rainforest countries does not feed its citizens. It leaves the country. For example, the United States annually imports more than 200 million pounds of meat each year from Costa Rica, El Salvador, Guatemala, Honduras, and Panama. As a direct result, the average person in those countries eats less meat per year than the average American house cat.

Cows produce almost 20% of the methane in the atmosphere, the number two greenhouse gas. It has been claimed that a single cow is reportedly capable of emitting as much as 100 gallons of methane gas a day. Fortunately, for those of us who share the planet with cows, this gas rises into the atmosphere. Unfortunately, once it's there, the gas contributes to the warming of the planet—the "greenhouse effect".

Methane is one of the major gases contributing to the greenhouse effect. Cows are not the only producers of methane. (And apparently most of what they produce is burped—much less is emitted through their bovine posteriors.) Other ruminants such as sheep also emit methane. Termites are also reported to be a producer, as are rice paddies, marshland, and the burning of forests. But there's no doubt that the more than one billion cattle on the planet are major methane producers.

Skip that hamburger and you've saved 55 square feet of rainforest. That's 55 square feet of vegetation that will continue to be a habitat for a multitude of tropical plants and animals instead of methane-producing cows. See? The responsibility all comes back to you.

> **Meatless Monday**
> www.meatlessmonday.org
>
> Recipes, health information and monthly promotions to encourage you to reduce your intake of meat and saturated fat.

Choose healthy foods

You already know what's healthy and what isn't. Sure, there are some gray areas. But there's little doubt that processed foods, and those filled with chemicals, are not as healthy as unprocessed, whole grain, naturally grown, chemical-free foods. That doesn't mean you have to be fanatic about it. Your food choices are yours, but when you're faced with the choice between a "healthy" food and a "less healthy" one, consider which is likely to improve your health.

> **Produce for Better Health Foundation**
> www.5aday.com
>
> Provides 5-a-day recipes and tips for getting your five to nine daily servings of fruits and vegetables.

Center for Informed Choices (CIFC)
www.informedeating.org

Advocates for a diet based on whole, unprocessed, local, organically grown plant foods. CIFC believes that: placing these foods at the center of the plate is crucial for promoting public health, protecting the environment, and assuring the humane treatment of animals and food industry workers.

Eat Well Guide
www.eatwellguide.org

Free national online directory for locating producers, grocery stores, restaurants, and mail-order outlets that offer sustainable meat, including organic. The site is organized by methods of production (antibiotic free, hormone free etc.), third party certification (such as organic) and source.

World's Healthiest Foods
www.whfoods.com

Foods that are nutrient-dense, whole, familiar, readily available, affordable, and taste good.

Sustainable Table
www.sustainabletable.org

Introduces the idea of sustainability and links food purchasing choices to health, protecting the environment, rural communities and animal welfare.

Seafood Watch
www.mbayaq.org/cr/seafoodwatch.asp

The Monterey Bay Aquarium's Seafood Watch helps you determine which fish are healthier choices.

SPECIALTY FOODS

There are many foods you can grow, or find, yourself, no matter where you live or how large your home. They'll add variety to your vegetable garden's produce, and save additional money at the market.

Grow sprouts

Sprouts are an easy-to-grow, high-protein and high-fiber, space-saving food. They're high in vitamin C and many B vitamins, and contain enzymes that aid digestion. Everybody should be growing sprouts.

Seeds that are frequently sprouted include alfalfa, mung bean, soy bean, sunflower and clover, but many others can be grown as well.

To grow them takes about 10 minutes a day, using supplies as simple as a quart glass jar, water and seeds. No matter how small your home, you're sure to have space to grow sprouts.

> **Growing and Using Sprouts**
> www.waltonfeed.com/grain/sprouts.html
> **Instructions from Walton Feed.**
>
> **How to Grow Sprouts and Wheatgrass**
> www.handypantry.com/grow.htm
> **Instructions on jar, tray and soil methods. Also offers prouting kits and seeds, and instruction DVD/Video.**
>
> **Sprouting at Home**
> www.cityfarmer.org/sprout86.html
> **Urban agriculture notes from City Farmer.**

Sproutman
www.sproutman.com
Wide variety of information and products.

SproutMaster
www.sproutpeople.com
Offers information, seeds, kits and more.

Find mushrooms

Mushrooms are nutritious, delicious, and much more. Although there are more than 70,000 species of fungi, only about 250 species are considered delicious. Since there are also around 250 species that can kill you, we recommend you first start out with an experienced mushroom person. Below you'll see the website for local amateur mycology clubs that can help you.

Fungi Perfecti
www.fungi.com
Company promoting radically new environmental uses for gourmet and medicinal mushrooms. Extensive free information. Highly recommended.

MykoWeb
www.mykoweb.com
Devoted to the science of mycology (the study of the fungi) and the hobby of mushrooming (the pursuit of mushrooms). Includes the "The Fungi of California" with photographs and descriptions of over 400 species of fungi found in California (and over 1800 total photographs).

North American Mycological Societies
www.mykoweb.com/na_mycos.html
Amateur mushroom clubs in the United States and Canada.

Tom Volk's Fungi
www.tomvolkfungi.net
Excellent resources with a very useful beginner's
introduction.

Forage for wild plants

Why shop for food when you can just pick it? Particularly
when it's everywhere. Just make sure it's in an area that hasn't
been sprayed or otherwise contaminated. Be certain that what
you're picking to eat you have absolutely identified as safe;
some deadly plants can look very similar to other safe plants.
Some plants can be eaten raw; others must be cooked.

If you're a city dweller, don't despair. You might even have
safe, edible food growing in a large city park. As with
mushrooms, it's important to eat only those plants you can
positively identify as safe. Common temperate zone plants
include berries, nuts, and plants such as dandelion, asparagus,
ferns and, if you live near the ocean, seaweed.

Edibility of Plants
www.wilderness-survival.net/plants-1.php
Information on what to eat—and what not.

A Field Guide to Edible Wild Plants [book]
Author: Bradford Angier
North American edible plants - where to find them, when
and how to gather them, and how to prepare them.

Edible and Medicinal Plants of the West [book]
Author: Gregory L. Tilford
Includes full color photographs of every plant in the
book.

Feasting Free on Wild Edibles [book]
Author: Bradford Angier

Guide to North American edible plants. Includes more than 500 recipes.

Identifying and Harvesting Edible and Medicinal Plants [book]
Author: Steve Brill

In wild (and not so wild) places.

The Illustrated Guide to Edible Wild Plants [book]
Author: Department of the Army

Produced by the U.S. Army.

The Neighborhood Forager [book]
Author: Robert K. Handerson

A guide for the wild food gourmet.

Stalking the Blue-Eyed Scallop [book]
Author: Euell Gibbons

On the immense variety of seafoods available on the ocean's edge. Hundreds of recipes.

Stalking the Wild Asparagus [book]
Author: Euell Gibbons

The classic book on foraging for edible plants in the wild. Includes hundreds of recipes.

The Wild Food Gourmet [book]
Author: Anne Gardon

Fresh and savory food from nature.

Raise small animals

They're not just cute when they're young; they're tasty. Chickens and rabbits require little space, and can be raised in most city (and certainly suburban) backyards. Your town may have ordinances allowing raising such animals for your own use. If they don't, that could change. Perhaps even faster if you push them.

Chickens have an additional feature that rabbits don't. The hens lay eggs, usually starting at around the age of 20 weeks and continuing for as long as three years.

Barnyard in Your Backyard [book]
Author: Gail Damerow

Beginner's guide to raising chickens, ducks, geese, rabbits, goats, sheep, and cows.

Chickens in Your Backyard [book]
Author: Rick Luttmann

A beginner's guide.

Beginner's Guide to Raising Chickens [video]
www.chickenvideo.com

Simple instructions for brooder preparation, unpacking mail-order chicks, treating chick health problems, moving poults into a hen yard, hen house options, flock management, how to spot common diseases and parasites and basic butchering methods.

Backyard Chickens
www.backyardchickens.com

Created to help others find the information they need to raise, keep and appreciate chickens.

Raising Rabbits for Fun and Food
www.rudolphsrabbitranch.com

Includes a primer on backyard meat rabbit raising practices.

Make cheese

Basic cheese making is simple and economical, and the results are delicious. Eat it yourself, give it away, barter it, or even sell it.

Soft cheeses such as ricotta or cottage cheese can be made overnight. Hard cheeses such as cheddar need to age for several months. Ingredients include milk, rennet (a digestive enzyme you can buy in the supermarket), and a starter such as buttermilk or yogurt.

How to Make Cheese
www.gourmetsleuth.com/cheeserecipes.htm

Recipes for making your own cheese at home - from Gourmet Sleuth.

Making Artisan Cheese [book]
Author: Tim Smith

Fifty fine cheeses that you can make in your own kitchen.

Making Cheese at Home
http://schmidling.com/making.htm

Basic instructions and recipes.

1...2...3...Cheese
www.dairygoats.com/hightor/Home%20Cheesemaking%20is%20easy.htm

Recipes and instructions from Ventura County 4H.

Fankhauser's Cheese Page
http://biology.clc.uc.edu/Fankhauser/Cheese/Cheese.html

Excellent site with instructions, photos and recipes.

COOKING

You probably already know how to cook. But there are ways of cooking you might not have tried that use less energy (and thus less money) and that provide greater nutrition and health.

Cook with solar energy

Solar cookers intensify the sun's heat to cook foods. With solar, you cook flavorful meals with free, non-polluting energy. It typically takes twice as long to cook with solar as it would with a conventional oven.

Cooking with solar can be totally free after the initial cost of building or buying a solar cooker. You can buy cookers for as little as $20 or make them yourself for a few dollars.

You can cook all year round, depending on the weather, in tropical regions and in the southern United States. Further north, you can cook whenever it is clear, except for the three coldest months of the year.

Solar Cookers International
www.solarcookers.org

Spreading solar cooking to benefit people and environments.

Solar Cooking Archive
www.solarcooking.org

A lot of information from Solar Cookers International. Includes free plans for making your own solar ovens.

Solar Oven Society
www.solarovens.org

Non-profit organization sells solar ovens to help support its activities in developing countries.

> **Sun Oven**
> www.sunoven.com
>
> Ovens for sale that are used around the world, including large ovens used by villages.

Eat more uncooked (raw and living) foods

Living (such as sprouts) and raw (fruit, vegetables, seeds, nuts, and grains) foods are said to have a much higher nutrient level than foods that have been cooked. Raw foods contain enzymes, which assist in the digestion and absorption of food. These enzymes are destroyed in the cooking process.

Raw and living foods should be organic, so that you avoid the toxins found in most conventional foods. Most people agree that organic foods also taste better.

By eating raw and living foods you avoid the use of energy in meal preparation. That means less cost to you and less use of fossil fuels by society.

> **Living and Raw Foods**
> www.rawfoods.com
>
> Frequently asked questions.
>
> **Raw Food Directory**
> www.buildfreedom.com/rawmain.htm
>
> Guide to books, magazines and websites.

Cook medicinally

Using herbs and spices for health is more than just drinking herbal tea. Although that's an excellent way to take advantage of herbs' healing properties, you can also integrate herbs and spices into most cooking recipes for health and healing support.

Examples are garlic as an anti-microbial and to lower cholesterol, onions for colds and as an expectorant, cardomom as an antiseptic, ginger for colds and arthritis, and marjoram for indigestion.

Culpeper's Herbal
www.bibliomania.com/2/1/66
Sixteenth century herbal classic.

Spices – Exotic Flavors and Medicines
http://unitproj1.library.ucla.edu/biomed/spice
Use of spices as medicine from UCLA.

Encyclopedia of Spices
www.theepicentre.com
Information on more than 40 spices.

Growing Medicinal Herbs
www.organic-gardening.net/articles/growing-medicanal-herbs.php
Growing and using herbs for health.

HerbKits
www.herbkits.com
Indoor herb garden kits [products].

HerbKits
www.herbkits.com/medicinal.htm
Indoor medicinal herb kits [products].

Medicinal Herb Package
www.heirloomseeds.com/herb2.htm
Package of seeds from Heirloom Seeds. [product]

FOOD STORAGE

Proper food storage can help food last a long time. Dried foods, such as beef jerky, dried fruits, or even dried vegetables, are popular and tasty. Canning your own food is not as common as it was fifty years ago, but is still done by millions of people. They can enjoy the taste of fresh food long after the season is over, and save money by buying bulk foods in season when they are at their lowest price.

Drying food

Drying food—dehydration—is usually a simple procedure involving little or no equipment, and will allow the food to last for extended periods of time. Foods can be dried in the sun (with or without a solar dehydrator), in an oven, or with an electric dehydrator.

Drying removes the moisture from the food so that bacteria and molds can't grow and spoil the food. The best temperature for drying food is 140°F. Higher temperatures will cook the food instead of drying it.

Fruit can be dried outdoors in the sun over a period of several days. Dehydrators, costing as little as $50 or less, speed up the drying process by lowering the humidity of the surrounding air.

Drying Foods
http://cahe.nmsu.edu/pubs/_e/e-322.html

Methods of drying foods from the College of Agriculture and Home Economics New Mexico State University.

Dehydration of Food
www.canningpantry.com/dehydration-of-food.html

Foods and how to dry them.

Canning food

Canned food can include fruits, vegetables, sauces, meats, and soups. Canning food is both simple and inexpensive. If you know how to boil water, you know how to can food. You can buy a cheap canner for $20 or less, and probably get free glass jars from friends or yard sales. You'll need rings and lids for the jars, but these are very inexpensive. Some fresh food, and an hour or two of your time, and you will have done it.

Canning 101
www.backwoodshome.com/articles/clay53.html
Simple instructions for canning.

Canning Food
www.uga.edu/nchfp/questions/FAQ_canning.html
FAQ from National Center for Home Food Preservation.

Keeping food cool without refrigeration

You don't necessarily need a refrigerator or freezer to keep foods cool long-term. For centuries people have preserved food in cool environments such as cellars, cold water (in containers), and by using the cooling effects of evaporation, in clay pots.

The key to food storage is lowering the temperature where the food is stored. You also want to minimize exposure to light and keep it in as dry (non-humid) an area as possible. Optimum food storage prolongs shelf life, nutritional value, taste, texture and color. Date all food containers and rotate, so that you're continually selecting from the longest-stored foods.

Cool Food Storage
www.inthewake.org/b1cool.html

Various methods including water immersion, cold rooms, root cellars, ice caves, and pot-in-pot.

Pot-in-Pot Cooling
www.rolexawards.com/laureates/laureate-6-bah_abba.html

A simple technique that can be used anywhere in the world.

Refrigerator Alternatives
http://groups.yahoo.com/group/RefrigeratorAlternatives

A Yahoo discussion group on energy-efficient home refrigeration, including traditional refrigerators as well as root cellars, cooling cabinets, brine solutions and much more.

Root Cellar Basics
www.waltonfeed.com/old/cellar4.html

From Walton Feed.

National Center for Home Food Preservation
www.uga.edu/nchfp

Many types of preservation for many types of food.

Prudent Food Storage FAQ
www.survival-center.com/foodfaq

Excellent and very comprehensive information.

ATTITUDE ADJUSTERS

Beer

Nothing quite quenches the thirst like a cold brew. When you make it at home, you can have real beer, as opposed to that mass-produced stuff. It's simple to make beer, though it takes some skill and experience to make *good* beer.

Brew Your Own
www.byo.com
The how-to homebrew beer magazine.

The Brewery
www.brewery.org
Total homebrewing information.

How to Brew [book]
www.howtobrew.com
Free online book.

Make Beer
www.instructables.com/id/E897F4SS6AEP28750F/
Complete instructions for making beer along with extensive step-by-step photographs.

The New Complete Joy of Homebrewing [book]
Author: Charles Papazian
Considered by many to be the bible of home brewing.

Wine

"I always cook with wine. Sometimes I even add it to the food." - *W.C. Fields*

Home winemaking has always been popular. And not everyone insists that it be Cabernet Sauvignon. Blackberry wine, dandelion wine, apple wine—there's no limit to what you can use as the basis for your creation.

A Quick Guide to Making Wine
www.homebrewmart.com/wineinst.html

28-day recipe for generic wine.

The Home Winemakers Manual
www.geocities.com/lumeisenman

Free online book.

Joy of Home Wine Making [book]
Author: Clem Stein

Even spice wines, herb wines, sparkling wines, sherries, liqueurs, and soda pop.

Making Wine from Rare Fruit
www.crfg.org/tidbits/makewine.html

Making Wines from Wild Plants
http://winemaking.jackkeller.net/plants.asp

With lots of recipes.

Roxanne's Fruit Wine Recipes
http://scorpius.spaceports.com/%7Egoodwine/
fruitwinerec.htm

Everything from apple jack to watermelon wine.

Winemaking Recipes
http://winemaking.jackkeller.net/recipes.asp

More recipes than you'll be able to make in several lifetimes.

> **Wine World FDW**
> **www.wineworldfdw.com**
>
> **An excellent site on making wine from a whole bunch of different things, none of them grapes. Highly recommended.**

Liqueurs

Man does not live by beer and wine alone. There are also liqueurs, originally crafted centuries ago by monks as healing elixirs. At least that's what they claimed.

Liqueurs, also called cordials, are sweet alcoholic beverages made from fruits, herbs, barks, seeds, spices, and flowers that are usually delicious and frequently even healthy.

Many liqueurs are best when aged for some months, but some can be ready in a few days, if you're really impatient.

> **The Alaskan Bootlegger's Bible [book]**
> **Author: Leon W. Kania**
>
> **How to make beer, wine, liqueurs and moonshine whiskey.**
>
> **The Art of Making Wine and Liqueurs**
> **Author: B. Sampson**
>
> **Step-by-step guide to home wine and liqueur making— from flower, fruit, and sparkling wines to sloe gin and cherry brandy. 100 recipes.**
>
> **Classic Liqueurs [book]**
> **Author: Cheryl Long**
>
> **The art of making and cooking with liqueurs.**
>
> **Cordials From Your Kitchen [book]**
> **Author: Pattie Vargas**
>
> **Easy, elegant liqueurs you can make and give. Recipes for fruit, nut, spice, coffee, and cream liqueurs, plus flavored brandies, rums, and vodkas.**

Liqueur
http://en.wikipedia.org/wiki/Liqueur
From Wikipedia.

List of Liquers
http://en.wikipedia.org/wiki/List_of_liqueurs
Information on more than 75 commercial liqueurs.

Liqueur Making
www.guntheranderson.com/liqueurs.htm
Principles and techniques.

Making Liqueurs and Cordials
www.liqueurweb.com
Excellent directory of resources.

Recipe Links
www.liqueurweb.com/links.htm
Recipe sites.

Coffee

According to the Whatcom Seed Company: *Coffea arabica* is easy to grow indoors, makes a very attractive houseplant, and if it likes you well enough it will even reward you with flowers and berries. A six-foot plant can produce two to four pounds of coffee a year. Grow in medium light, or filtered or indirect sunlight. Use a rich, acid soil kept moderately moist. Peat moss in the potting mix will help provide acid conditions. Ideal temperatures are between 60° F and 85° F. Give the roots room to grow. Hardy to 28° F.

Coffee Arabica
http://seedrack.com/02.html
Coffee seeds from Whatcom Seed Company.

Coffee Growing at Home
www.coffeeresearch.org/coffee/homegrowing.htm
Step-by-step instructions.

Coffee Substitutes
www.coffeeresearch.org/coffee/homegrowing.htm
From Civil War days.

Growing Coffee Arabica at Home from Seed
www.sweetmarias.com/growingcoffeeathome.html
Good instructions and photographs, but the author isn't
very optimistic about success.

Grow Your Own Herbal Tea
www.hgtv.com/hgtv/gl_herbs/article/
0,1785,HGTV_3595_2045629,00.html
Information on growing common herbs for tea.

Tobacco

Yes, we know it's unhealthy. Or at least the mass-produced commercial products are. But what if it's organic, without pesticides and all those chemicals? Tobacco has medicinal value, makes an extremely valuable ornamental plant and flower garden specimen, and is used to make one of nature's finest biodegradable, all natural pesticides.

Coffin Nails
www.coffinnails.com
Grow and smoke your own tobacco.

Growing and Processing Tobacco at Home [book]
Author: Jim Johnson
www.seedman.com/Tobacco.htm#1
A guide for gardeners. Tax-free and chemical-free
tobacco. And it's legal.

Tobacco Plant Information
www.boldweb.com/greenweb/nicoinfo.htm

Planting and raise, curing, other non-smoking uses, and U.S. policy.

Tobacco Plant Seeds
www.boldweb.com/greenweb/tobacco.htm

Enough seeds for 25 or more plants.

Health

It's a cliché to say that without health you have nothing, but it's still obviously true. And the healthier you are, the better your life is likely to be. If you take responsibility for your own health, you can bring about remarkable results. The tips we offer here can bring about a dramatic improvement in how you feel, yet they cost nothing.

Walk 30-60 minutes a day

(See page 19.)

Get more sleep

More than 70% of Americans of all ages suffer from sleep deprivation. One of the best things you can do is get more sleep, and a more regular sleep. Based on what time you have to get up in the morning, set a bedtime at least seven hours prior to the time you rise. (After a while, try to extend this until you're getting eight hours of sleep at night.)

The amount of sleep needed depends on the individual, so experiment. Studies show that most Americans think they're getting enough sleep, and those same studies also show that they aren't.

Having trouble sleeping? Visit www.insomniatips.net for a number of ideas on how to deal with insomnia and get to sleep.

Simple Tips to Help You Get to Sleep
www.insomniatips.net

Free home and folk remedies to deal with insomnia and help you sleep.

Eat better

We don't have to tell you what you should be eating more of, and what you should be eating less of. You already know. But don't try to change all at once. That way lies failure.

Tomorrow add to your daily diet just *one* thing that you know you should be eating but haven't been eating, either because you don't really care for it or because you "just don't get around to it". Next day add another food. Keep doing that each day, experimenting with a different food.

After one week, eliminate one food each day that you know you should really eat less of, or not at all. Do that as well for one week, again with a different food each day.

When we suggest this, we don't mean keep adding (or subtracting) an additional food each day. We mean just experiment, one a day less, or one a day more. After you've done this for a couple of weeks, see how you feel. Then see which foods you can, and want to, add—or remove— permanently.

Living to 100 Life Expectancy Calculator
www.agingresearch.org/calculator/

See where your present lifestyle might get you.

Cooperative Health Insurance
www.healthdemocracy.org

An interesting proposal to establish cooperative health coverage in the United States.

Where There Is No Dentist [book]
Author: Murray Dickson

A community dental care manual designed to help people care for their teeth and gums.

Where There Is No Doctor [book]
Author: David Werner

A community health care manual. Vital information on diagnosing and treating common medical problems and diseases, giving special emphasis to prevention. Includes sections detailing effective examination techniques, home cures, correct usage of medicines and their precautions, nutrition, caring for children, ailments of older individuals and first aid. Translated into more than 90 languages.

Try Alternative Health Techniques

Millions of people use natural and alternative methods of healing. Not all of the methods work, at least not for everyone. And there no doubt exist quacks, frauds, and pseudo-science treatments. But it's your body. You decide.

You'll find a selection of the more popular methods at this site.

Alternative Health
www.beyondpeak.com/health-beyondpeak.html
A variety of techniques from aromatherapy to yoga.

Air

Ideally you're living in a location that has lots of fresh air. However, many people aren't able to live in such a place. You may live or work in a building with no circulation, and filtered recycled air. Or you may live in a city with bad pollution, from automobiles, factories or other causes.

There are still things you can do. Probably the most important is to keep your living and working space as healthy as possible. The best and easiest way to do this is with plants and trees.

Purify air with houseplants

B.C. Wolverton, an environmental consultant and retired NASA scientist, describes in his book "How to Grow Fresh Air" how houseplants filter toxins from the air in your home. Plants break down the chemicals commonly found in the home, including those from paint, plastics, cleaning supplies, and synthetic carpets.

Plants such as Boston ferns and lady palms are among the best and are easy to care for. The ferns remove formaldehyde and the palms are excellent for removing ammonia. Spider plants deal with benzene, which is found in house paint. Plants are also excellent air purifiers in offices, which are frequently closed systems with no natural ventilation.

How to Grow Fresh Air [book]
Author: B.C. Wolverton

50 house plants that purify your home or office.

Plant trees

Trees absorb carbon dioxide and produce oxygen. They also lead to lower air temperature, provide shade and shelter, cut down noise pollution, improve water quality, and stabilize soil. That's a lot more than we humans do. The least we can do is plant more trees.

A single tree can remove as much as 25 pounds of carbon dioxide a year. An acre of forest can absorb up to 5 tons a year. This country's forests—which are decreasing at nearly one million acres a year—can remove more than 1.5 billion tons of carbon dioxide a year.

If one out of every two Americans planted one tree by their home or business, we could save $4 billion in energy costs and reduce carbon dioxide emissions by 18 million tons a year. The shade from three trees around your home could reduce your air-conditioning needs up to 50%.

According to the U.S. Department of Agriculture, the net cooling effect of a young, healthy tree is equivalent to 10 room-size air conditioners operating 20 hours a day. The U.S. Forest Service says that trees properly placed around your home can reduce air conditioning needs by 30% and save 20-50% in heating costs. Their attractiveness also increases the market value of your home, and being around them relieves stress.

When you're planting trees, consider fruit and nut trees. If they're appropriate for your tree location, you might as well get food as well as shade.

Tree People
www.treepeople.org

Non-profit organization offers extensive information, including how to plant a tree.

The Urban Tree Book
Author: Arthur Plotnik

An uncommon field guide for city and town.

Drive less

Drive your car as little as possible. Carpool, walk, bicycle, use public transit—anything to reduce the amount of carbon dioxide released by the burning of fossil fuels.

Water

Water. We use too much and, increasingly, have too little. It's probably our most precious resource and we squander it. The average person in the United States uses between 100 and 250 gallons of water a day. It's possible—and you may have no choice—to get by on a lot less.

Showers account for 2/3 of the average water heating cost, and 20% of water usage. Take shorter showers and you'll save money and energy. You should at least have low-flow shower heads. Also try turning the shower off while soaping up, then back on to rinse.

Your toilet should be low-flow. Ideally, it would be a composting toilet using no water at all. Waterless urinals are also available, although more often seen in commercial establishments.

More advanced, but effective, water-saving techniques include using graywater (from sinks, showers and washing machines) for watering gardens, and *xeriscaping*—using local, drought-tolerant plants that may need no watering at all.

H2ouse Water Saver Home
www.h2ouse.org

A guide to conserving water from the California Urban Water Conservation Council.

Low-flush or compost toilets

Toilet tanks should use no more than 1.6 gallons per flush. Toilets are the largest water-wasters in the home, wasting gallons of water with every flush. If you can't put in a low-flush toilet, at least add plastic displacement bags to your toilets. (Don't use bricks. They just break apart and cause problems.)

Stop leaks

Leaks can waste many gallons of water a day. Check for toilet leaks, as well as leaky faucets and water pipes. For toilets, put a drop or two of food coloring in your tank. If the color appears in the bowl, you've got a leak.

Xeriscaping

Xeriscaping means using native plants that are at home with your local climate conditions. They're natural, and they need no watering.

Use Less Water and Save

Here are some normal household uses of water, how much water they use normally, and how much less they use if you try to conserve.

Shower – Normal, 25 gallons – Wet down, soap up, rinse off, 4 gallons.

Brushing teeth – Tap running, 2 gallons – Wet brush, rinse briefly, one-quarter gallon

Shaving – Tap running, 10 gallons – Fill basin, 1 gallon.

Dishwashing – Tap running, 15 gallons – Wash in dishpan or sink, 5 gallons.

Automatic dishwasher – Full cycle, 16 gallons – Short cycle, 7 gallons.

Washing hands – Tap running, 2 gallons – Fill basin, 1 gallon.

Flushing toilet – Normal, 3.5-5 gallons – Low-flow toilet, 1.6 gallons.

Washing machine – Full cycle, top water level, 40 gallons. Short cycle, minimal water level, 25 gallons.

Capture rainwater

Capturing rainwater is called "rainwater harvesting". It basically means water delivered directly to your home from the skies at no charge. You just have to catch it, clean it, and store it. Assuming you have enough rainfall in your area, it's a way to become self-sufficient—or to at least supplement your municipally-supplied water.

> **Rain Barrel Guide**
> www.rainbarrelguide.com
> **How to use rain barrels for water collection. Excellent overview and specifics.**
>
> **Raincatcher**
> www.raincatcher.org
> **Harvesting natural rainwater to quench the world's thirst.**
>
> **Garden Watersaver**
> www.gardenwatersaver.com
> **System uses any container for rainwater collection. [product]**
>
> **Natural Rain Water**
> www.naturalrainwater.com
> **Information, products, and how to make a rain barrel.**

Reuse your graywater

Graywater is the water from dishwashing, laundry, showering and bathing. While no human wants to drink it, plants are happy to get it. You can set up a system that will save and recycle that water to be used in your garden.

> **Graywater Central**
> www.graywater.net
> **All about graywater.**

Purify your own water

If, unlike hundreds of millions of people around the world, you're lucky enough to have access to water, you still need to make sure it's safe.

There are a number of devices and chemicals you can buy to purify water, ranging from hand-held filters to iodine tablets or hydrogen peroxide.

Here's an incredibly simple—and free—way of disinfecting water using solar radiation and plastic bottles.

Solar Water Disinfection (SODIS)

The Solar Water Disinfection (SODIS) process is a simple technology used to improve the microbiological quality of drinking water. SODIS uses solar radiation to destroy pathogenic microorganisms which cause waterborne diseases.

SODIS is ideal for treating small quantities of water. Contaminated water is filled into transparent plastic bottles (PET bottles are best) and exposed to full sunlight for six hours.

1. Wash the bottle well the first time you use it.
2. Fill the bottle to the top and close the lid.
3. Place the bottle on a corrugated iron sheet or on the roof.
4. Expose the bottle to the sun from morning until evening for at least six hours.
5. The water is now ready to drink.

Solar Water Disinfection Process
www.sodis.ch

For more detailed information.

Water

Colloidal silver

A centuries-old technique for purifying water is silver, used frequently these days in high-tech air and water purification systems, such as recirculating air on aircraft.

> **Blue Future Filters**
> www.bluefuturefilters.com
> Low-tech slow sand filters [products].
>
> **Ceramic Water Filter**
> www.potpaz.org/pfpfilters.htm
> Low-tech colloidal silver-enhanced ceramic filtration and purification of water from Potters for Peace.
>
> **Silver Ceramic Water Purifiers**
> www.purifier.com.np
> Low-cost, high-performance water purification.
>
> **Solar Water Disinfection Process**
> www.sodis.ch
> An incredibly simple—and free—way of disinfecting water using solar radiation and plastic bottles. This information needs to be spread all over the world.
>
> **Treatment of Water to Make it Safe for Drinking**
> www.cdc.gov/travel/water_treatment.htm
> From the Centers for Disease Control.
>
> **Water Purification**
> http://en.wikipedia.org/wiki/Water_purification
> From Wikipedia. Includes overview of water treatment methods, other purification techniques, and portable water purification.
>
> **Water Purification for the Traveler**
> www.artoftravel.com/10water.htm
> Obtaining safe water, filters vs. purifiers, selection criteria, comparison of filters.

Water Treatment FAQ
www.1stconnect.com/anozira/SiteTops/water/
waterFAQ.htm

Storage and purification.

WaterCure.com
www.watercure.com

Website of the author of "Your Body's Many Cries for Water".

The Wonders of Water
www.watercure.com/wow/wonders_of_water.html

Healing uses of water.

Your Body's Many Cries for Water [book]
Author: Fereydoon Batmanghelidj

You are not sick; you are thirsty.

Bottled Water: Pure Drink or Pure Hype?
www.nrdc.org/water/drinking/nbw.asp

Research results on high cost and health hazards of bottled water.

Transportation

Moving from one location to another can, and should, be enjoyable, not just a battle or chore. Commuting creates wear and tear on the driver, the driver's vehicle, and the environment. People in developed countries, particularly in the United States, are used to hopping in their car and driving anywhere, even if their destination is only a few short minutes away.

Why not try some other ways of getting around?

Walk

It's free and healthy. (See page 19.)

Ride a bike

It's a low one-time cost, and very healthy. (See page 21.)

Use public transit

If your community has public transit such as bus or light rail, use it. If it doesn't go where you need it to go, join with others to get it expanded or changed.

Electric/gas scooters

Scooters aren't just fun; they're inexpensive transportation. They get great mileage, using very little fossil fuel. A gallon of gas can can take you 50 miles or more. New scooters will cost you anywhere from $800 to $4,000, though it's possible to spend as much as $10,000.

Moped Army
www.mopedarmy.com
Blog headquarters for moped clubs.

Motor Scooters
www.motorscooters.com
Comprehensive information and sales.

Scooter
http://en.wikipedia.org/wiki/Scooter
Wikipedia article.

Vespa
www.vespa.com
Official Vespa company site.

Electric Bikes
www.electric-bikes.com
Practical transportation for errands and short commutes.

Buy carbon offsets

Carbon offsets are environmentally beneficial actions that balance out the harm we cause by emitting carbon dioxide (CO_2) by travel, or through other causes. These beneficial actions are generally tree-planting or investing in renewable energy. They're basically "good karma" balancing out "bad karma". Look at carbon offsets as a kind of "environmental sin tax" or the equivalent of buying *indulgences* in the Middle Ages. You pay your penance and you get to keep doing the bad karma. (You might want to look at that, too, however, and determine how you can reduce your carbon emissions throughout your daily life—and *still* support tree-planting and renewable energy.)

Various websites let you buy "offsets" after calculating how much CO_2 you have to balance out to become "carbon neutral". For example, your "share" of an airline flight from San Francisco to New York is estimated to be as much as 1,000 pounds of CO_2.

Carbonfund.org
www.carbonfund.org

Individuals and businesses can reduce their carbon footprint and support climate-friendly projects.

Native Energy
www.nativeenergy.com

A privately-held Native American energy company. Their carbon calculator lets you calculate the carbon emissions resulting from your travel by auto, bus, rail or air. You can then buy "carbon offsets", offsetting those travel CO_2 emissions by financially supporting green energy projects that wouldn't happen otherwise.

TerraPass
www.terrapass.com

Make your driving carbon-neutral by balancing your emissions with a TerraPass.

Compressed work week

The best way to avoid driving to work is to avoid going to work at all. Compressed work schedules (such as a four-day, 40-hour work week) can eliminate commuting altogether one day a week for many employees. Companies with such programs report less absenteeism, fewer late employees, and less use of sick leave.

In a compressed work schedule program, employees work a full-time schedule in fewer days, by working more hours a day. The day off can be the same for all employees, vary or rotate regularly—but most employers choose to assign days off to ensure adequate coverage. The most common compressed schedules are:

"4/40" - A 40-hour week consisting of four 10-hour days and three days off a week

"9/80" - 80 hours worked over two weeks, consisting of eight 9-hour days, one 8-hour day and five days off.

Where can compressed work schedules best be used?

Compressed work schedules work best where employees require minimal face-to-face contact with other employees, where set-up/tear-down time or shift changeovers are necessary (e.g., hospitals or manufacturing), or where work functions are not disrupted by staff reduction.

Compressed Work Weeks
www.valleymetro.org/Rideshare3/9CWW
List of benefits.

CARS

Most environmentalists are focused on "environmentally responsible" ways of fueling automobiles. In other words, their goal is to keep everyone driving cars but to do it in a more efficient and "green" manner.

Some see the issue differently, and realize that one of our core problems is our society's dependency on the automobile. They say that what is needed is a dramatic change in our transportation systems and our design of cities, towns and especially our suburbs. They also note the huge amount of energy and resources needed for the manufacture of automobiles, and the equally huge amount of land area (much of it formerly agricultural land) required for highways, roads and parking.

That said, we will still suggest ways you can make your use of automobiles "better". But we urge you to find ways to lessen, or even avoid, the use of *any* type of automobile.

In fact, selling your car and using all other forms of transportation (foot, bike, bus, train) could be the best move you could make. You'll stop polluting the atmosphere, you'll save large amounts of money (gas, repairs and maintenance, insurance), you'll probably get more exercise, and you'll be able to enjoy life at a slower-pace, paying more attention to your surroundings and its inhabitants.

Car costs

The U.S. Department of Labor says that car costs are the second highest expense for the average U.S. household, about 17% of expenses. That's almost the same as food and health care combined.

The Real Costs of Car Ownership

www.bikesatwork.com/carfree/cost-of-car-ownership.html

Calculate your own monthly car costs based on all related costs over the year. You can also see how that money could instead be used for college or retirement savings, or for a home mortgage.

If you absolutely need your own car to get to work, why not change jobs? Or move to a location that no longer requires a car to get to work? A car is a major burden; you'll be surprised how liberating it can be to get rid of it.

Improve your fuel efficiency

There are many things you can do to get better fuel efficiency with your existing car.

1. Use your car's air conditioner as little as possible. Air conditioners can decrease your mileage as much as 20%. They're more efficient on the highway, much less efficient in stop-and-go city driving.
2. Drive at a steady speed. Speeding up and slowing down greatly increases fuel usage. Avoid jack rabbit starts, and plan ahead to slow down at traffic lights and stop signs.
3. Drive at moderate speeds. Most cars get their best mileage somewhere around 50-55 miles per hour. Going faster increases wind resistance and decreases fuel economy by as much as 6% for every five miles an hour over your optimal speed.
4. Keep your car well maintained. Keep your car in the best possible condition with regular tune-ups, and you'll get the best possible mileage. A badly maintained engine can use as much as 50% more fuel and produce 50% more pollution.
5. When you see a hill coming up, start accelerating before you get to it. It takes much more fuel to accelerate going up a hill than on a level road.
6. It's better to turn off your car than to let it idle for a long period of time. More than 10 seconds of idling uses more gas than you'll use to restart.
7. Most cars these days don't need a long warm-up time. Start driving slowly as soon as you can. The car will warm up along the way.

- Measure your tire pressure monthly. Keep the tires at the proper level and you'll get better gas mileage and a smoother ride. You can improve your gas mileage by around 3.3 percent by keeping your tires inflated to the proper pressure. According to the U.S. Department of Energy, under-inflated tires can lower gas mileage by 0.4 percent for every one pound per square inch drop in pressure for all four tires.
- Replacing a clogged air filter can improve your car's gas mileage by as much as 10 percent. Your car's air filter keeps impurities from damaging the inside of your engine. Not only will replacing a dirty air filter save gas, it will protect your engine.

Buy a fuel-efficient car

Go for the most fuel-efficient car you can find. Currently, hybrids (electric/gas) are at the top of the fuel-efficiency charts. We suggest the likelihood that a hybrid or other high-mileage car will have a high resale value; in fact, once people start realizing how high gas prices can go, your hybrid could appreciate in value far beyond what you paid for it.

> **Hybrid Cards**
> **www.hybridcars.com**
> **Comprehensive information and links.**
>
> **Zap SmartCar**
> **www.zapworld.com/cars/smartCar.asp**
> **Not a hybrid, pure gas-driven. But great mileage.**

Carpool

Carpool to work, or even on errands, whenever possible. Talk to co-workers about sharing driving and see if your company has a policy of subsidizing carpooling, since it requires fewer parking spaces in the company parking lot.

> Most municipalities and transit agencies can give you information about carpool networks, where you can find people going to the same area in which you work.
>
> eRideShare.com
> www.erideshare.com
>
> A free service for connecting commuters or travelers going the same way.

Car sharing

Some communities now offer *car sharing*, where you have use of a car whenever you need it, but you don't have to maintain it.

With car sharing, you pay for a car, van or truck only when you use it. Cars are available 24 hours a day, and you can reserve by phone or Internet. You never pay for repairs, insurance or monthly parking.

> CarSharing Network
> www.carsharing.net
>
> Find out which cities around the world have car sharing.
>
> Car Sharing
> http://en.wikipedia.org/wiki/Car_sharing
>
> From Wikipedia.
>
> CarSharing.us
> http://carsharing.us
>
> Blog hosted by car sharing pioneer Dave Brook.
>
> What is Carsharing?
> http://ecoplan.org/carshare/general/basics.htm
>
> Carsharing and its benefits.
>
> World Carshare Consortium
> www.worldcarshare.com
>
> Worldwide news and links, and online forum.

Use biodiesel

Biodiesel is a processed fuel for diesel engines derived from biological sources, usually rapeseed or soybean oil. Because biodiesel is much cheaper than gasoline, many people are now making their own biodiesel, or at least buying it, for their diesel engine vehicles.

Collaborative Biodiesel Tutorial
www.biodieselcommunity.org
How to make biodiesel.

Biodiesel
http://en.wikipedia.org/wiki/Biodiesel
From Wikipedia.

Biodiesel America
www.biodieselamerica.org
Book, news and information.

Biodiesel Basics
www.gobiodiesel.org/index.php?title=BiodieselBasics
Benefits and drawbacks.

Collaborative Biodiesel Tutorial
www.biodieselcommunity.org
Learn how to make biodiesel.

Diesel
http://en.wikipedia.org/wiki/Diesel
From Wikipedia.

Electric vehicles

Full-size electric-only automobiles are not currently available, particularly since General Motors killed the EV1, but smaller electric forms of transportation are becoming more and more popular.

Battery Electric Vehicles
http://en.wikipedia.org/wiki/Battery_Electric_Vehicles
From Wikipedia.

EV World
www.evworld.com
Electric and hybrid vehicles.

Light Electric Vehicles
www.electric-bikes.com/lev.htm
From bikes and small scooters to one-person cars.

Segway
www.segway.com
The Segway Human Transporter.

ZapWorld
www.zapworld.com
Electric ATVs, scooters, and bikes.

Buy carbon offsets

(See page 126.)

Money

EXPENSES AND INCOME

Cutting down on your expenses saves money in many ways, and paying off debt goes even further since you're escaping from interest rates.

Cut down on your expenses

It's even better than increasing your income because you don't have to pay additional income and sales taxes.

- Cut down on your use of electricity, gasoline and natural gas. This book is filled with suggestions on how to do that. Follow them, and you'll enjoy some major savings.
- Grow at least some of your own food. (For information on starting a home garden, see page 74. For a community garden, see page 85.)
- Buy less, sell more. Buy only what is absolutely essential, or what you *really*, really want. Look around your home and see if there are things you don't need — there is always someone, somewhere who is willing to buy those things.

Pay off debt

If you carried out action #1 above, you may be able to use some of the money you saved through cutting expenses to start paying off debt. Since much of any debt you have is liable to be credit cards and bank loans, the money you avoid having to pay in interest through lowering your debt is much more than you'd receive if you simply invested the money you saved from cutting expenses.

For example, if your credit card requires that you pay an 18% annual interest, paying off some or all of that card is the equivalent of investing the amount you paid at 18%. You'll have a hard time finding any investment that pays even close to that.

Best advice? Stop buying on credit unless it's an absolute emergency.

Here are some interesting figures about debt.

♦ In 2004, the credit card industry made $43 billion from fees for late payments, over-limit, and balance transfer.

♦ In 2005, total American consumer debt was $2.2 trillion, with an average of $11,840 per household.

♦ Average U.S. household credit card debt increased 167% between 1990 and 2004.

♦ In 2005, the average interest rate on credit cards was 14.5%.

♦ In 2005, the rate of personal savings in the United States was negative .5%, dropping below zero for the first time since the Great Depression.

♦ In 2004, 45% of U.S. cardholders were making only minimum payments on their credit card debt.

♦ As of 2004, a typical credit card purchase (including interest) is 12-18% more than if cash were used.

♦ In 2005, 2.39 million U.S. households filed for bankruptcy, a 12% increase over 2004.

♦ During the three years prior to 2005, 30 million Americans (40% of homeowners) refinanced their mortgages, with over half of them applying the proceeds to their credit card debt.

♦ In 2004, the average personal wealth of a 50 year-old American was less than $40,000—including home equity.

Find a self-employment opportunity

Self-employment is no guarantee of financial security, but neither is the fact that you're currently employed. Look for work that can supplement or replace your current income (or lack of it). The one thing you can count on about the economy is that things are going to keep changing. Your job is to guess what those changes might lead to, and be there to meet them with new job skills, tools and whatever you need to take advantage of the opportunities.

♦ Do a self-inventory

Look at the skills, talents and experience you currently have and seek ways to turn those into an income.

♦ Study

Consider what skills you could learn in order to become self-employed, then take courses, read books and find other ways to learn them.

♦ Learn on-the-job

Get an entry-level job in the business you'd like to learn, or see if you can apprentice (even with no pay) with someone who already has these skills.

Invest in yourself

If you're looking for somewhere to invest, why not start at home? Spend some money on things that will make you and your family as self-sufficient as possible. Buy seeds and equipment to start a garden. Buy bicycles. Buy compact fluorescent bulbs to replace your incandescent bulbs. Take classes that will increase your useful knowledge and skills.

Buy property for a larger garden. Buy food storage equipment such as canning supplies and dehydrators. Buy solar panels or wind turbines. Buy equipment and supplies you'll need to set up your own business. Take classes in alternative health techniques.

Invest in local business

If you still have money you'd like to invest, consider assisting one or more local businesses. There are undoubtedly existing local businesses, or people wanting to start a business, that need a loan to start up or expand, or for other purposes. Some of these people may be unable to qualify for a standard bank loan, even though they have solid business plans. If you feel they're worth investing in, your loan, even if small, can make a significant difference.

You'll find it's possible to make loans locally at an interest rate higher than a bank will give you and, for the person borrowing the money, at a rate lower than they would get from a bank. It's a win-win for both of you.

For ideas on how this might work, take a look at Prosper.com, a website that brings borrowers and lenders together. They offer people-to-people lending, in which you can be the sole lender, or join with others so that each lender provides part of the loan needed by the borrower.

Through such investing, you're helping your community's economy as well as receiving a fair return on your investment. Making small investments like this is similar to, and based on, the programs initiated by the Grameen Bank, which began in 1976 in Bangladesh to give micro-loans to the poor who were unable to qualify for regular bank loans. The principle is similar here, although the monetary amounts are much greater.

> **Prosper**
> www.prosper.com
> People-to-people lending.
>
> **Grameen**
> www.grameen-info.org
> Micro-loans for the poor in Bangladesh.

BARTER

Barter is simply trading one thing for another. And, in fact, it doesn't even have to be a *thing*. It can be a skill, a service, or even information.

Barter can save you money, and increase your interaction with members of your community. It also lessens your need to make money to "get things."

Now is a good time to begin to *demonetize*. Lessen your dependence on the financial system and its dollars, and increase your skills and relationships so that you can get the things and services you need by exchanging other things, services of your own, knowledge or anything else which might be considered of value. You'll learn that members of a community can help one another without needing to use pieces of paper (with pictures of dead presidents) to validate the mutual help.

Economic sustainability isn't just about money; it's about knowledge, skills, and cooperation. It's about being able to create and produce your own goods, either yourself or within your community. Nevertheless, some stuff is useful, and it doesn't hurt, no matter how good or bad the times, to have supplies of necessities around the house.

Remember that bartering doesn't have to be only in a one-on-one relationship. A mutual bartering system can be even more effective at the neighborhood or community level.

Running a barter network can also be an excellent form of self-employment. Barter is often confused with systems such as community currency. The difference is that barter involves only goods and services. Community currency, or systems such as LETS, involves either locally-printed currency or a computerized system to keep track of exchanges.

(For closely related information, see Local Currency, page 61.)

Barter with friends, neighbors and local businesses and services

You should have no problem finding people you already know to barter with. It's really just an extension of giving away things you don't need. Local businesses might have more need of services rather than things. Ask and see what they can use.

Join, or start, a barter network

Ask around to see if there is already a barter network in your community. There may actually be several. While there are statewide and nationwide barter exchanges, it's best if you can keep most of your bartering at the local level. It helps build community, and it cuts down on transportation expenses and use of fossil fuels.

Develop a skill or product that you can use to expand your barter opportunities

Do an analysis of the skills you have already. If necessary, take a class to improve current skills or acquire new ones. Analyze the needs of people and businesses with whom you'd like to barter, and see if you can fill any of those needs.

Barter
http://en.wikipedia.org/wiki/Barter
From Wikipedia.

Small Lodge, the Great Depression, and Christmas
www.srmason-sj.org/council/journal/dec00/dodson.html
Small Masonic lodge in rural Virginia established a barter system to help its community through the hard times of the 1930s.

Barter - Relevance and Relation to Money
www.ex.ac.uk/%7ERDavies/arian/barter.html
Is barter still relevant in the modern world? Links and history.

How to Barter
www.u-exchange.com/barter101.asp
Advice for online bartering but useful for face-to-face bartering as well.

Energy

COOLING

There are a number of ways to keep your home cooler— without the cost and energy use of air conditioning.

Use window coverings

Close drapes, curtains, blinds and windows on south (in the northern hemisphere) and west-facing windows on hot days. This is particularly important with south-facing windows but should be done with all windows. At night, open them up to let the cool air in (if there is any).

Use ceiling fans instead of air conditioning

Although they don't actually lower the temperature of the air in the room, they lower the *perceived* temperature. Fans move the air around creating a wind chill effect that makes you *feel* cooler because of increased evaporation of moisture on your skin. You'll save a lot of energy by using fans instead of air conditioning.

Remember that since they cool *you* and not the air, there's no point in having them on when no one's in the room.

Shade your home

Use trees, deciduous plants and/or awnings to shade your home and windows. For more, see page 117.

♦ If you must use air conditioning, keep your thermostat set no lower than 77° F. when you're at home, 85° F. when you're away from home. Your air conditioner uses three to five percent more energy for each degree below 75° F. Set it to 77° F. for the most comfort at the least cost.

♦ Turn off your furnace pilot light during the warm season. You'll save both money and energy. For safety, your utility company will probably do this at your request.

LIGHTING

Lighting is a major need in most homes, but it's also a major expense. There are many easy ways you can cut down on costs and still keep the lighting you need.

Use compact fluorescent bulbs

(See page 17.)

Turn off lights when you don't need them

Leaving lights on in an unoccupied room is a waste of electricity and money. Turn the lights off when you leave, and back on when you return. Despite what many people believe, the act of turning a light on uses very little electricity. It really does save electricity and money to turn them off.

Get up earlier and go to bed earlier

Get up at sunrise and go to bed earlier in order to take advantage of natural light. Natural light saves energy and is easier on your eyes, you'll be more in sync with natural rhythms, and you'll save money on lighting.

HEATING

More than half of the energy used in the average home is on heating and cooling. Remember that your goal doesn't have to be to heat the entire home; it's simply to heat the people in it.

Dressing warmly can be a major way of dealing with the cold; putting on a sweater is cheaper than raising the thermostat. Devices such as radiant heaters are also good because they use much less energy since they heat people, not the air in the room.

Set your thermostat lower than normal

Keep your thermostat set no higher than 68° F. during the day. Wear warm clothing if necessary. Set the thermostat to 55° F. before going to bed at night.

Replace/clean your furnace filter regularly

A clean-flowing filter will be more effective and require less energy than a dirty filter.

On sunny days, use passive solar heating

Keep the drapes open on south-facing windows to let the sun shine in. At night, close the drapes to retain indoor heat.

Ceiling fan

During the winter, set your ceiling fan to run *clockwise* at low speed. This produces a gentle updraft, which forces warm air near the ceiling down into the occupied space.

Stay warm at night

We lose most of our heat at night through our head and neck. In addition to warm blankets and warm pajamas or other night clothes, wear a nightcap. Socks or other comfortable foot coverings will keep your feet warm as well.

POWER

Power is what makes just about everything work. Producing it on a large scale requires lots of fuel, such as coal, oil and natural gas. If there's a shortage of any of those fuels, serious problems can, and will, begin.

But you can produce your own energy, in ways that are sustainable, economic (at least in the long run), and most importantly, available.

Use less

The three most important areas in your home where you can cut electricity use and save money are:

Lighting

Replace incandescent bulbs with compact fluorescent bulbs (page 17).
Turn off lights when you're not using them .

Heating

Turn down your heating thermostat (page 24).
Turn down your water heater (page 24).

Cooling

Turn up your air conditioner thermostat (page 143).

Saving Electricity
www.michaelbluejay.com/electricity

An excellent website with very specific information on how to save money on your home appliances and systems.

Kill-a-Watt

An "electricity usage monitor" that measures the amount of electricity consumed by household appliances—even when they're not actually being used but are simply plugged in. A great way to see where you can reduce your electricity consumption. [product]

Generate your own

Depending on your climate and location, there are a number of options for generating your own power. If you're fortunate, you might be able to combine two or three of these methods to ensure year-round power.

Solar energy

Solar is the most common form of renewable energy. The sun doesn't have to be shining brightly to produce energy, but it helps.

Solar requires a high initial expense because of the cost of photovoltaic cells, which convert sunlight into electricity. If you're fortunate, you live in an area where your state or utility gives rebates, or at least loans, to install solar.

Real Goods
www.realgoods.com
The pioneer in home solar energy.

Real Goods Solar Living Sourcebook [book]
Author: Real Goods
The classic information catalog.

Small Solar Electric Systems
www.eere.energy.gov/consumer/your_home/electricity/
index.cfm/mytopic=10710
From the U.S. Department of Energy.

Wind energy

Wind is better than solar if your area has enough reliable wind. Wind turbines of various designs turn from the force of the wind and generate electricity. A number of firms have the goal of producing low-cost wind turbines for the home that are the size of a satellite dish. Unfortunately they're not perfected yet.

Small Wind Electric Systems
http://www.eere.energy.gov/consumer/your_home/electricity/index.cfm/mytopic=10880
From the U.S. Department of Energy.

Wind Energy Basics [book]
Author: Real Goods
A guide to small and micro wind systems.

Wind Power, Revised Edition [book]
Author: Paul Gipe
Renewable energy for home, farm, and business.

Hydro energy

Hydro, or water, energy is best known from the large dams that block rivers and generate huge amounts of energy from the water's flow—or fall. Micro-hydro, which produces up to 100kW, is the mini-version of hydro for the home. It's the most efficient form of sustainable energy generation and is ideal if your home is right next to a year-round stream.

Pico-hydro generates up to 5kW of electricity. Low-cost (less than $US 20) water turbines from China are currently very popular in rural areas of Vietnam.

Micro-Hydro Power Systems
www.eere.energy.gov/consumer/your_home/electricity/
index.cfm/mytopic=11050

From the U.S. Department of Energy.

Pico Hydro
www.picohydro.org.uk

Network promoting small hydro systems up to 5kW.

All About Hydraulic Ram Pumps [book]
Author: Don Wilson

The device that can pump water from a flowing source of water to a point higher than that source using the force of gravity rather than power.

How to Live Without Electricity - and Like it [book]
Author: Anita Evangelista

Live off the grid but still have power, water, heating, and refrigerated food.

Power with Nature [book]
Author: Rex A. Ewing

Highly-recommended book on solar, wind, micro-hydro, heating house and water and pumping water.

Use a solar battery charger

With a solar battery charger and chargeable batteries, all you need is sunshine to keep all your battery-operated devices working. They're available online and at a variety of local shops such as hardware and camping stores.

Buy a wind-up or solar-powered radio

There are a number of radios on the market that are charged up by turning a hand-crank, or by using a small solar panel to charge the battery. Some models include both methods. You'll never again need batteries or an electrical outlet to listen to the radio.

FreePlay
www.freeplayenergy.com
The pioneer in wind-up, solar and rechargeable technology.

C. Crane
www.ccrane.com
Excellent source of radios and other electronics.

Stuff

REDUCE / REUSE / RECYCLE

Use the Three Rs—Reduce, Reuse, Recycle—when dealing with *stuff*.

Reduce

Reduce the amount of stuff that you buy. Simply use less. Buy only what you need—or what you *really*, really want. Buy tools, appliances, furniture, clothing and other items that are designed to last for many years. Avoid buying things designed to be quickly used and thrown away. Seek out items that were made with natural materials under appropriate labor conditions.

"Reduce" is also referred to as "precycling". Avoid stuff in the first place. Wherever possible, avoid packaging and containers. If you have to get them, get containers that are recyclable. Avoid prepackaged and prepared foods. Buy whatever you can in bulk to save packaging and reduce costs, and prepare your meals from scratch.

Precycling means avoiding waste (and often saving money) by making good environmental decisions at the store.

Select products in recyclable containers such as paper, cardboard, glass and aluminum. Avoid disposable and single-use products unless absolutely essential.

Avoid plastic containers whenever possible. If you have no choice, make sure that the recycling symbol (three arrows in a circle) is on the packaging.

Reuse

Avoid disposable items. Buy items that can be used over and over; if not by you, then by someone else. Buy items that can be maintained and repaired so that their useful lifetime can be extended.

Recycle

When you finally have no need of something, pass it on to someone else who can use it. If it is past the point where it can be used, recycle it so that its materials can be reused in some other form.

Recycle everything made from metals, plastic, wood, fibers, glass or paper. Someone, somewhere, probably has a use for it. Clothing, furniture, household items, tools and toys can all be used by someone else, particularly if they can get them for free.

Books can go to the local library for use or resale. Usable items can be given to local charities and thrift shops, taken to local materials recycling depots, or simply put in front of your house with a big sign that says "Free" (if your local regulations allow).

SHOPPING

Shopping is a way of life for many people, but there are ways —particularly at the supermarket—that you can could down on purchases and expenses, with a minimum of suffering.

Avoid prepackaged products

A significant percentage of the cost of many products is the packaging. The more you can avoid packaged products— particularly frozen foods, snacks, prepared mixes, and the like —the more money you save and the more you avoid the need for recycling (page 150).

Carry your own cloth shopping bags

Carry your own sturdy cloth or net bags for shopping. You will no longer have to make the "Paper or plastic?" choice (which, in essence, is "Tree or oil?"). It avoids any need for recycling, and cloth bags are a lot stronger than paper or plastic bags. Most grocery stores sell them; some even give them away.

Skip the middle of the supermarket

In most supermarkets, that's where all the prepared foods and snacks with additives, preservatives and heavy sugar are. On the perimeter are the real foods: meat, dairy and produce. Venture into the middle only for such essentials as flour, cooking oil, spices, cleansers and the like.

Avoid chain stores

Shop locally (page 58). If you still have them, patronize local specialty stores such as butchers, fishmongers, green grocers, hardware stores, office supplies and the like.

Sustainable Living Checklist

Here's a list of suggested key actions you can take to live more sustainably. Check off an item whenever you've done it (or have begun the new habit of doing it regularly).

Home

- ☐ Use compact fluorescent light bulbs
- ☐ Walk daily
- ☐ Ride a bike daily
- ☐ Plant a garden
- ☐ Install low-flow toilets
- ☐ Install low-flow shower heads
- ☐ Stop leaks
- ☐ Start a compost pile
- ☐ Use a clothesline
- ☐ Plant trees
- ☐ Use a hand mower
- ☐ Share housing

Family

- ☐ Family dinners
- ☐ Family entertainment
- ☐ Family meetings

Neighborhood

- ☐ Organize your neighborhood
- ☐ Start neighborhood sharing
- ☐ Plant a neighborhood garden
- ☐ Take down the fences

Community

- ☐ Patronize "Third Places"
- ☐ Buy from locally owned businesses
- ☐ Use local currency
- ☐ Get involved in community affairs

Food

- ☐ Support local farmers
- ☐ Eat organic
- ☐ Grow sprouts
- ☐ Grow herbs
- ☐ Make beer or wine

Health

- ☐ Get more sleep
- ☐ Purify air with houseplants

Transportation

- ☐ Drive less
- ☐ Use public transit
- ☐ Carpool
- ☐ Car share
- ☐ Buy carbon offsets

Money

- ☐ Cut down on expenses
- ☐ Pay off debt
- ☐ Barter
- ☐ Find a self-employment opportunity

Power

☐ Turn down water heater temperature
☐ Use a solar oven
☐ Use ceiling fans instead of air conditioning
☐ Shade your home
☐ Turn off lights when not needed
☐ Replace/clean furnace filter

Shopping

☐ Precycle
☐ Recycle
☐ Use a cloth shopping bag
☐ Avoid chain stores

NOTES

Sustainable Living Index

Visit This Book Online

All links in this book to websites, books, DVDs, products and other information are available at:

www.sustainablelivingbook.com

The online links are checked and updated regularly to ensure their accuracy and functionality.

You can also order additional copies of this book at the above website.

7/08

961661